HORSE TRIALS
AND
TRIBULATIONS

Julian Seaman

Drawings by Anne Pilgrim

PELHAM BOOKS

Stephen Greene Press

PELHAM BOOKS/STEPHEN GREENE PRESS

Published by the Penguin Group
27 Wrights Lane, London W8 5TZ, England
Viking Penguin Inc., 40 West 23rd Street, New York, New York 10010, USA
The Stephen Greene Press, 15 Muzzey Street, Lexington, Massachusetts 02173, USA
Penguin Books Australia Ltd, Ringwood, Victoria, Australia
Penguin Books Canada Ltd, 2801 John Street, Markham, Ontario, Canada L3R 1B4
Penguin Books (NZ) Ltd, 182–190 Wairau Road, Auckland 10, New Zealand

Penguin Books Ltd, Registered Offices: Harmondsworth, Middlesex, England

First published 1990

Typeset in Linotron 12/14½pt Korinna Medium by Goodfellow and Egan Ltd, Cambridge
Printed and bound in Great Britain by
Butler and Tanner, Frome

ISBN 0 7207 1932 1

A CIP catalogue record for this book is available from the British Library.

Contents

1. If at first you don't succeed — give up

Before you decide to take up three-day eventing in any of the various capacities which will become apparent, it's probably worth discovering exactly what the sport is that you are letting yourself in for.

It was once described by an American General, Tupper Cole, as 'the ultimate test of an officer courier who got through or died'. Are you still interested?

In its early days, it was restricted to cavalry officers, but those restrictions no longer let you off the hook.

There are, however, many advantages of knowing something about, or participating in eventing. Not only are the well-documented Royal connections worth a few social Brownie points, but it is actually one of the very few sports where Britain has continually done rather well. This may be because, unlike so many other sports which we invented and taught the world how to beat us, eventing in its present form has developed from various international ideas all cobbled together.

For those who want to compete, it is a sport for the brave, but you don't have to be rash enough to take this drastic action to become 'an expert'. In fact, it is probably an advantage not to, as no one will ever know how cowardly or hopeless you might have been. With the help of this book, you will, instead, be able to pass endless critical comment on those who fall into ponds, or scatter coloured poles with gay abandon.

If you really want to risk your reputation and actually ride, this book should point you in some of the right directions also.

A three-day event is the pinnacle of more watered-down versions of the sport, also known as horse trials. It has variously been described as a 'pentathlon on horseback', or, uncharitably, 'a test for a Jack-of-all-trades and master of none'.

Its military origins stem from when horses played a major role in warfare. A horse needed to be controllable, full of stamina, fast, and in one piece at the end of the day.

The first phase of the competition is dressage – a strictly tedious test of the horse's stopping, starting, steering and posing abilities. A set test of movements, not unlike compulsory figures in skating, has to be performed. For both horses and riders on the less brave side, dressage has become a sport in itself, and at the top end, the clever movements involve strange acrobatics which were originally designed to perform such tasks as booting your assailant off his horse. At an even higher level, dressage is not a sport at all, but what the protagonists term a 'Classical Art', which means they prance around to music wearing

'Its military origins.'

silly hats without the pressure of competition, and seeing their pictures on dishcloths from Vienna. Eventing types should be in awe of these techniques (or at least pretend to be), but can safely ignore too close an involvement with these pretensions.

It is the all-action glamour of the speed and endurance phase which excites the eventer. Dressage is the necessary evil, and we could speculate that had the intrepid gentlemen of the Light Brigade learned how to control their mounts properly, they may not have charged at all!

The endurance phase is the second part of a three-day event. The first bit is innocuous enough, and involves a happy trot of a few miles through the countryside.

In deference to Eurospeak, all measurements are now metric, and each marked kilometre can be covered in a leisurely four minutes. Even full-time dressage riders could do this bit. But then the fun starts. Competitors arrive at a prefabricated steeplechase course, and although they go round individually against the clock, can pretend they are jockeys for a couple of circuits. The pretence doesn't really compare, since the speed, although at a gallop, is considerably slower than in a race, and also, of course, there aren't a dozen other lunatics hurling themselves at the jumps at the same time.

The next phase, again part of the endurance factor, is a slightly longer trot through the countryside before ending up at a hub of activity called 'the box'. This is a large pen, roped or fenced in, where there is a compulsory ten-minute break and the horses are checked to see if they are fit to carry on.

Then comes the main part – the 'what it's all about' phase. Ahead lies a course of about four and a half miles (work out your own metric equivalent) scattered with as many as thirty enormous, complicated, spectacular and seemingly well-nigh impossible jumps, involving rails, ditches, banks, ponds, hedges and any other type of immovable object that the course designer has dreamt of putting in the way. These jumps are solid and not designed to 'knock down'. (Keep remembering that you need never indulge in these horrors, and still become an expert.)

Even after riding through the finish flags of this assault course, there is more to come. Day three.

Going back to the army origins, this final part is to test that the rider hasn't over-exerted his horse in the heat of battle, and that it can still be ridden the following day.

Before this phase, the horses are again checked for soundness and then complete a twisty, if not 'Horse of the Year Show sized', jumping course over knockdown coloured fences.

If after this description eventing sounds extremely

complicated to follow as an armchair supporter with a six pack – it is.

The scoring system works on a penalty basis, but to start with, the dressage, which is judged on individual set movements as a plus mark, has to be subtracted from the optimum score to obtain a penalty. (There is also a fearsomely involved multiplication factor too, but since almost no one in the sport understands it, you don't need to either.)

The trotting about the country bits hardly ever cause penalties, as they are judged purely on arriving at the destinations inside an easily-achievable given time. Likewise with the steeplechase, though refusing a jump, or most expensive of all, parting company with your steed can spoil a nice day out.

'Parting company with your steed can spoil a nice day out.'

It is the cross-country where you are most likely to come unstuck, with so many opportunities to make a Horlicks, but the show-jumping can be the most frustrating, because all the heroics of the previous two days can be thrown away by one careless clip of a coloured pole.

Disappointments to an event rider are more than just an occupational hazard – they are a certainty. The saying goes that horses are great levellers – greater levellers than a steamroller. Competitive riding is a 'character building' occupation – which, translated, means that you spend most of your time in gloom and desperation, kept going by the uncertain possibility that one day you might get it right.

But the riders have to be optimists. They see it the other way round. Any minor success makes all the heartache worthwhile.

If after all this you still see yourself as a budding star, the next chapter could help. But eventing can be thoroughly enjoyed from *terra firma*, with no risks to life or limb and often not to the pocket either.

If you have no intention of proving whether you could be the 'officer courier who got through or died', never fear. A good knowledge of the jargon, and an involvement with the sport in any minor way will enable you to be part of the 'Eventing Scene'.

Once a member of that scene, you will realise that you have joined an elitist set – so make the most of it. For a start, you have chosen a horse sport. Doesn't it sound better to say 'I was an official (however minor) at Badminton' than 'I was a bouncer at the Cockney Darts Classic'. (Real style would have you win the Cockney Darts Classic and also be an official at Badminton – or perhaps be one of the more well-endowed ladies who won Badminton and was a bouncer at the darts match.)

Having chosen horses instead of, say, ocean-going sailing as the sport you wish to follow, why eventing instead of the other equestrian sports?

Why not 'the Sport of Kings' – **Racing**? For a start, racing is an 'industry' not so much a 'sport'. It is designed for you to lose money at the bookmakers, however knowledgeable you may be. Your chances of landing six-figure sums as an owner are far outweighed by the day-to-day training and entry fees (unless you were born in the Middle East), only a handful of jockeys or trainers make a decent living out of it at any given time, and the local drunk in any bookmakers' office will already know more about the game than you will ever learn if you're starting now. Racing is split between those 'in racing' and those who lose money 'going racing'. Eventing is a much more intimate sport, where you can quite easily become involved 'in horse trials'.

Dressage is for those who have lost their 'bottle' or never had it on the competitive side; for those enthusiasts who are happy to spend whole days watching others going round in neat circles and criticising each wrong flick of a fetlock. At least for eventers it's only a small part of their repertoire.

Polo, although relatively exciting as a spectator sport, is, I'm afraid, beyond your reach if you want to become more involved than just treading in divots at half-time. To play, you need strings of 'ponies' and to be involved in the social side not only requires gold card facilities at your champagne supplier, but also the almost inevitable risk of losing your spouse.

Eventing may be expensive and carry some of the same risks, but to a lesser degree, and your value for money in an upmarket environment is much better.

Show jumping once had quite a lot going for it, and there are still many opportunities to become 'involved' without either spending a fortune or having to actually jump a seven foot, red plywood wall at Wembley. But if it's 'image' you're after, forget it. If, however, you still have romantic notions of running away with the circus, it may be for you.

Eventing may have an established circuit, but it hasn't become a circus (yet).

The relatively new sport of **Carriage Driving** is a form of eventing with carriages, and the atmosphere is similar in its camaraderie and opportunities for the non-combatant (as opposed to the incompetent) to play a large part.

The only trouble is that it was almost single-handedly invented in Britain (by Prince Philip). This has, as usual, and in a very short space of time, allowed overseas teams to learn the sport and continually beat us.

Foxhunting, though not in the accepted sense of the word, a competitive sport, is, despite difficulties on many fronts, more popular than ever.

You can become a keen eventing supporter and hold whatever views you like about hunting. But to be part of the horse scene, you must know something about 'the chase'. You will be forgiven for disliking hunting provided you actually can pretend to understand something about it.

If someone approaches and says enthusiastically, 'I see X has taken Daisy hunting to sharpen him up before Badminton,' don't give a diatribe about why you think hunting is wrong, say, 'What a stupid risk before such a big event,' or, conversely, 'Just the thing for him, it's what I'd do'.

Eventers may always be labelled Jacks-of-all-trades. The racing world is more professional, the horses are faster and the majority of jockeys are paid, expert professionals, and the profession is directly linked to the betting public.

The showjumpers leap much larger fences than the eventers, for considerably more money, and the dressage riders can perform much more sophisticated manoeuvres than most top eventers could dream of.

But eventers are the Kings and Queens of riding across country.

As I said the cross-country phase can be up to four and a half miles. This is why horse trials are for you, even as a spectator.

Imagine the acreage which could accommodate such a course. With over one hundred and fifty trials in Britain a year, some venues may be better than others, but a lot are held in some of the most picturesque parts of the country.

You can go for the day and pretend that you are a private guest walking the grounds and seeing action at the same time.

If you have perhaps sensibly decided to become involved in eventing on the passive side, this manual should help you achieve that ambition. If you want to become a sponsor, organiser, jump judge, dressage judge, owner, steward, groom, trainer, course builder, journalist, broadcaster, announcer, paid administrator, general dogsbody or even professional spectator, you can find out in the later chapters.

If, on the other hand, you are still hell-bent on becoming an active eventer yourself, read on from here.

<u>Reasons</u>
<u>to event</u>

1. It's upmarket.
2. You can wear lots of different clothes.
3. Girls compete on equal terms with men.
4. You can't have a proper job.
5. You compete in great locations.
6. It's one sport where Britain still does well.
7. It's custom-built for a Jack-of-all-trades.
8. You can wear long leather boots, use whips and spurs in public and not get arrested.

<u>Reasons</u>
<u>not to event</u>

1. It's prohibitively expensive.
2. Horse sports are statistically high in the danger league.
3. Becoming a horse bore is even worse than becoming a golf bore.
4. If you get involved in horse maintenance, you and your clothes will smell.
5. Also, your hands will soon resemble those of a pneumatic drill operator.
6. You will have to ride in all weathers.
7. Just when you think you are about to become a star, your horse will fall to pieces.
8. Even in the horse world, pure dressage riders will think you can't ride dressage, proper showjumpers ridicule your efforts, jockeys mock your attempts on the steeplechase course, foxhunters think you are too competitive, polo players will despise you for not being as rich as them, and competitive cross-country riders will think you mad to bother with the other disciplines.

2. 'A horse, a horse, my kingdom for a horse' (Richard III)

So you really want to become a champion event rider? Well you've been warned, but here goes.

There are several routes to this ambition, and although it is almost certainly getting more difficult to achieve, there are more avenues to follow. That most of them turn out to be cul-de-sacs mustn't put you off.

As previously explained, the sport was once open only to army officers. (At the Berlin Olympics, the gold-medal-winning German rider had to be promoted from the ranks to allow him to compete.) It was only open to men for a long time.

However, once cavalry officers stopped riding horses and took to driving tanks instead, it seemed only natural for eventing to open up to civilians and even female civilians. So *you* are eligible. Horse trials is one of the few sports where men compete on equal terms with the women – and for reasons which may become apparent, the women (or 'Amazons' as eventing girls are referred to in the Continental press), now outnumber the men in the sport by a huge margin.

This example should not put you off by its restrictions, since if you have decided to become an eventer you can pick up the plot wherever your circumstances allow you to join it.

The *ambition* needs to be sparked off in the first place. If you have spent your early years being taken to see Arsenal, you may have dreams of becoming a footballer, or if you go to 'Holiday on Ice' every Christmas, perhaps a Jayne Torvill or Christopher Dean.

If, however, at an early age you have been to watch Badminton, that is where the fantasy will rest.

A useful tip at this stage for fathers – never take your children to Badminton. If the little darlings persist with this dream, it is going to cost you an arm and a leg. There is no point in giving figures, as they will already be higher as you read this.

Ideally the budding star has an indulgent mummy and daddy who live in 'the country' (even if poor father has to catch the 8:15 from Basingstoke every day). It helps if either parent has ever ridden, but not essential.

Step one usually happens to the girls, not the boys. On Christmas morning, the five-year-old child is taken out into the garden to see what Santa Claus has brought: a little, furry, brown and white bastard who answers to the name of Trigger. 'Ideal first pony', the advertisement said, as the screaming child is led down the lane with her brother following on the much more suitable present of a BMX bicycle.

If Santa's gift isn't instantly rejected, the next step is the
local riding school. Once a week, the Volvo will pull up at
Miss Rathbone's Establishment. Half a dozen teenage girls
will be ambling about with wheelbarrows, or manicuring
(manuricuring?) the steaming muck heap.

'Ideal first pony.'

Our future star will then have one hour's tuition from one
of Miss Rathbone's working pupils (a euphemism for an
adolescent whose parents actually pay for her to be a
slave). Whether you are five, or sixty-five, the principles of
riding are the same, so it might be helpful here to include a
technical passage to help all you aspiring eventers.

<u>**These principles of 'equitation' are dead easy to grasp.**</u>

1. The horse is considerably bigger than you.
2. Its brain is about the size of a golf ball.
3. If it wants to do something which you don't, it will win.
4. Horses *weren't* originally designed by God for you to sit on.
5. That's why you will fall off.
6. While trying to stay on, you will discover muscles which you didn't even want to know existed.
7. The day after your first ride you will not be able to walk.
8. All you have to do is relax.
9. Good point — how can you relax if you're terrified?
10. You can't.
11. If you're completely out of control, try anything to stay on board and trust that 'golf ball brain' doesn't want to kill himself as well.

Easy Rider

So how do you ride? There are all sorts of complicated ways of getting onto the beast in the first place, but as a beginner it's best not to attempt a John Wayne vault. Trying to mount in the traditional manner, by putting a foot in the stirrups, can lead to all sorts of embarrassment if you choose the wrong foot and end up sitting back to front.

Your instructor may offer you a 'leg up', which requires you to bend a knee and trust her to hoick you into the saddle. You are more likely, however, to be thrown straight over the horse and land in a heap on the far side – very undignified. No – find a mounting block (originally designed for dowager duchesses) and quietly ease yourself into place.

You are now 'mounted' and can look down on mere pedestrians.

What do you do now? Well, in terms of basics, it's much easier than driving a car.

You will have noticed that attached to the beast's mouth on both sides is a connecting strap. Grab it with both hands. This strap, 'the reins', is both your brakes and steering.

'Riding is simple: right for right.'

Acceleration is achieved by a simultaneous boot to the ribs with both legs. Riding is simple: boot to go; pull left for left; right for right and just pull like hell on both to stop.

This system usually works, but occasionally the little golf ball rattling around in your mode of transport has other ideas. At least in a car (apart from the more sophisticated

Japanese models), you don't have to deal with a brain, however small.

This is where psychology comes in. Don't fight the inevitable. If your horse is taking you at high speed towards the M25 against your will, pretend that's where you wanted to go. Only bale out when you can see the whites of the eyes of a Belgian pantechnicon driver. Presumably your steed wanted to 'go' that way.

But back to becoming a star. Your first riding lesson as a child goes well. In an indoor riding school, with mother looking on, you have been going round on the lunge – a long strap held by the instructor, attached to the pony's nose, so that the pupil can go round and round in circles, with no worry about steering.

The instructor gives a flattering verdict, 'You've got a very good seat', to ensure that next week's lesson will be booked.

Now it is time to become a member of The Pony Club (Brownies with rich parents) and the first meeting or 'rally'.

The brown and white fluffball is eventually persuaded to enter the seventh-hand trailer behind the Volvo and a morning's riding with similar little darlings continues. New instructors try to tell you basically the same story, only to be told that 'at Miss Rathbone's we do it this way'.

Next stop is the first competition: the local gymkhana. You have been entered in three races. The sack race, the trotting race and the bending race. What is bending? You may ask: weaving in and out of poles at a flat out gallop. Mother suddenly has ambitions of her darling appearing on TV in the victorious team at Wembley.

Sadly you fail to qualify for any finals at the gymkhana and burst into a frustrated tantrum. ('It was Trigger's fault, he *wouldn't* turn left when I wanted him to.' Cf: riding lesson.)

Now aged eight and having learned to jump (sit there

and let the pony do it), there is a nearby meet for children, of the local hunt.

Before you move off, the Master gives a little pep talk to the assembled crowd, and one or two 'aunty' figures attach themselves to the less confident.

All the Pony Club friends are riding as well, and since it is half-term, even some of the boys at prep school are there, impressing the others with stories about how they fooled matron that they had 'flu and got off games for a week.

When the hounds actually catch a fox, you arrive at the scene with your 'aunty' and in the old days would have been offered the (dubious) accolade of being 'blooded' – having the fox's blood smeared on your cheeks, and being given one of its feet, or 'pads'.

After hunting, the next stop is Pony Club Camp. Having said that the Pony Club is spoilt Brownies, being a Pony Club mother is the same as being in the WI, but with a daughter who rides.

Camp as row of tents

Pony Club Camps are held in the summer school holidays, when up to forty little dears are left with their ponies to the tender mercies of the group of adult saints who have volunteered to organise and instruct.

The trailers pulled up by the family saloons arrive at the camp site and out spill countless buckets, grooming kits, camp beds, sleeping bags, shovels, haynets, children and ponies. Everything, including occasionally the children and ponies, is name-tagged in the ridiculous hope that the inventory of kit will still be the same at the end of the week.

The children will have been organised into rides of about eight, according to their age and ability.

On the first morning's mounted inspection everyone is

'Everything is name-tagged.'

usually surprisingly well turned out (there are prizes to win at the end of the week for such things). Almost certainly mother will have polished all the tack and boots, and at this stage even the jodhpurs are clean.

Pony Club Camp is complete 'Thelwell' country: mini children mounted on borrowed clod-hopping giants; gangly adolescents who have grown nine inches in as many months, who need rollerskates on their boots as they spin around on their outgrown Shetland ponies, and the inevitable spoilt brats with their tailor-made champion show ponies which have won rosettes at Wembley, but won't jump a stick.

'Pony Club is complete "Thelwell" country.'

Quite a few boys, on parade from prep school, put in a reluctant appearance, and the more enterprising of these will bring two sets of kit with them. One for inspection, and polished by mummy, and one for actually using.

Basically, all the children hate doing boring old dressage, riding round in ever-decreasing circles, but their ponies would drop dead if they just galloped about all day. This is where the instructor has to con his group into believing that the 'schooling' is going to lead to some pre-arranged equestrian mayhem.

Pony Club Camp is designed to ensure that the children learn how to look after their ponies. This of course is a fearsome bore to anyone, and not to be recommended (although it is suggested that no one can become 'a complete horseman' without a good knowledge of stable management). This is of course complete nonsense, but if you want to become a champion eventer it might be useful to know what someone else is doing to look after your horse while you rightly continue to enjoy life.

3. Stable relationships

Stable management guide: (in a stable condition)

Unless it had escaped your notice, horses and ponies are
not domestic animals. However, for some peculiar reason,
horse lovers keep their beasts shut up in stables for the
majority of the time. This leads inevitably to a hygiene
problem – muck. Don't worry too much about this, since it
will be someone else's problem, but the stables have to be
'mucked out' twice a day.

   As muck goes, horse's muck is about the least offensive.
A good deal better than cowpats and way in front of
doggy-dos. The traditional bedding for horses is straw,
although modern alternatives include wood shavings or

shredded copies of *The Sun*. (A bit more muck on its pages won't make a great difference.)

To muck out all you need is a wheelbarrow and a pitchfork. The conveniently-designed droppings roll easily into the barrow, allowing you to toss the surplus bedding back into the stable. You do, however, have to dig a bit deeper to remove the damp areas.

With the barrow full, you march majestically to the muck heap, where you fork your load with precision, tidy the edges, stand back and admire. A trim muck heap means a well-run establishment. Once a month, the local mushroom farmer will ruin your 'castle' with his mechanical grabber and you have to start again.

Feeding If your horse is in a stable he obviously can't eat grass. Therefore you are going to have to feed him. Unlike your pet pooch, your horse is a confirmed 'veggie'. It's no use taking a bin liner to the local Tandoori and asking if they can fill your neddy bag. Horses eat muesli: bran, oats, concentrated grass pellets; everything, in fact, apart from the raisins. This, they are offered on average three times a day, but by way of a mid-meal snack they can chomp at a bunch of hay. They only really drink water, but gallons of it, so unless you have invested in an automatic drinks dispenser, the buckets will need checking several times a day.

Grooming This has got to be the most boring task. Dobbin is big – there is a lot of surface area to cover and all of it has to be meticulously brushed at least once a day. For this you will need a grooming kit.

A grooming kit
Dandy brush This isn't what Beau Brummell used in front

of his mirror, but more like something you (or again your staff) would clean the kitchen floor with.

It removes the mud, sweat and tears from the previous exertions. It's the universal brush.

Body brush This is what you tell everybody you use. Much softer than the dandy, it needs to be used with more force, accentuating the myth that it has massaging qualities. ('Real' grooms swear by them.) All this activity leads to equine dandruff, which is why a body brush has to be used with a –

Curry comb A good trick question is: where on a horse do you use a curry comb? – you don't. A curry comb is a peculiar-looking tool involving a square of metal with serrated teeth attached to a trowel handle, whose only use is to scrape the dandruff off the body brush. Three sweeps with the brush, one scrape on the comb: this ritual can last for over half an hour – I'm told.

Hoof pick Every Boy Scout has something to remove stones from horses' feet. Every Swiss Army penknife has a similar attribute. But horses' hooves get clogged daily with earth and gunge, so this blunt metal hook is essential.

Tail bandage About ten feet long, and two inches wide, this is not a veterinary item, but used purely to keep your beast's tail looking as if it had just left Vidal Sassoon's.

Hoof oil This is the equine version of nail varnish. Reputed to have a beneficial effect, this creosote-type concoction, when applied by brush to the four feet, can give a misleading air of good maintenance.

How to really ponce up your horse

For some reason it has now become accepted practice to
coiffure a horse or pony before showing classes, dressage,
jumping and even racing. This requires the groom (not
you) to be able to plait.

If left to nature, horses' manes (the hairy bit down their
necks) would reach their knees, and their tails would bush
out at the top and sweep along the floor. Equestrians,
however, like to 'pull' manes and tails. This is equivalent to
plucking your eyebrows. The mane and tail can then be
hairdressed into respectability.

'Equestrians like to "pull" manes.'

Plaiting the mane means grabbing an odd number of bunches up the horse's neck and securing them with rubber bands. (An even number just 'isn't done', and only the Continentals have more than nine or eleven.) You then plait each bunch, roll up the article into a ball and stitch it into place.

Plaiting the tail is a different, and quite unnecessary matter. But if you really feel you need the added bonus, start weaving the top hairs into each other, work down the bone, then work it into a regular plait, fold it in and stitch it up.

'A "chequer board" on the horse's bum.'

After all this, there is one more piece of icing to the cake: a 'chequer board' on the horse's bum. In the old days, this meant carefully using a small comb to brush against the grain. It's much easier now. You can buy plastic stencils and achieve an effect without any design training. A sensible entrepreneur could make a fortune out of Velcro plaits for shaved (hogged) horses, and slip-on plaited tails.

Now you know all you need to know about stable management. In fact, you would probably best forget the last section, and your groom will know it anyway. Let's get back to your equestrian education.

4. 'Each little flower that opens'

You have survived three years of Pony Club Camp, only having been sent home once for organising a raid on the next dormitory, and you still want to be a champion eventer. What is the next stage?

Well, let's face it, Trigger is now too small for you, even if you did win the bucket-jumping contest last weekend. Daddy has got to fork out for another star pony, take mother on an expensive holiday as a present for looking after Trigger, and accept that for the rest of his days he will have to pay for equine muesli.

The new pony arrives with glowing references from its vendors. It has been consistently placed in the area Pony Club horse trials team. At long last you could represent your Club in the eventing team . . . next stop Badminton.

Trigger is given to your reluctant younger brother as 'Bigger' is installed in the best stable.

Bigger terrifies the life out of you. You can't control him, steer him, or even stay on him, but daddy reminds you that he is already a 'champion' and it will be all your fault if he doesn't win again. Spoilt tears are wasted, because the ambition for greater things has taken over daddy as well.

As a keen budding eventer, you will now have to start taking your training more seriously. Ordinary riding lessons must be replaced with dressage lessons and 'schooling' over jumps. Children's first ponies don't do dressage, but tend to jump most obstacles without any help and often with considerable hindrance from the riders. The second pony, with luck, will also jump with ease, but can be persuaded to do a bit of dressage.

Hours must now be spent training the pony to keep its nose in and generally bend its neck in the direction it's supposed to be going, stop when it's told to without opening its mouth, break into walk, trot and canter exactly when told to by the rider, and act as if butter wouldn't melt in its mouth.

This is a long process. Lessons probably happen about once a week, but practice has to happen daily. The major drawback with horses and ponies is that they can't only be brought out to play when the rider's whim dictates. (This is now the time to buy a set of golf clubs, a tennis racquet, a dinghy, or, if going cross-country is your thing, a trials bike.)

Before the first Pony Club horse trial, vital match practice can be gained from entering small competitions in each of the three disciplines: dressage, show jumping and cross-country (hunter trials).

Dressage shows The Pony Club and the ruling body, The British Horse Society, have a series of tests to suit horses and riders of every ability. They are designed to last about four minutes at the more novice level, and up to about eight for the more advanced. There is one drawback – they have to be ridden from memory.

The performing arena is a rectangle of white boards with lettered markers in strategic places where changes of gait and direction are required. Eg. Enter at A (trot), halt at X, proceed to C, turn right, M canter, B circle right . . .

No one seems to have any idea how the letters were chosen, although X is understandably the middle spot. A is the entrance gap on one of the short sides, and the letters go round the rectangle AKEHCMBF. Quite impossible to remember, but this might help: *All King Edward's Horses Could Manage Big Fences*. Easy now?

Opposite A at C is the judge sitting in a car. When your turn comes, you go round the outside of the boards till the horn toots, and then commence the memory test. After your entrance, all tests require you to stop at X and 'salute' the judge. Drop a hand and nod your head. (Until recently boys would raise their hats, but since harnessed hats are now compulsory for Pony Club, removing the space helmet would take too long. This is just another indication of slipping standards of courtesy.) What all riders must do at this stage is to smile as sweetly as possible. The judge won't smile back, but it might be worth the odd extra mark. Giving a two-fingered salute at the end of the test is unlikely to enhance your reputation, even if that particular judge gave you a bad mark last time, despite your smile.

Show jumping There are lots of opportunities to have a go at this at the numerous little local shows round the country. There are classes to suit all levels of competence, age, ponies' height, and ambition.

During the winter, these shows are often held in indoor riding schools. Whatever the weather, the class can take place. But a word of warning. Your trailer will be parked in a mud bath; the practice area will be a cinder-covered swamp with two jumps and twenty people trying to jump them; someone else's father will have raised the height way out of your range; over one hundred people have entered your class so you have to wait an hour before you can compete in the warmth of the school; you will knock the last pole off the last fence, which means you can't go through to the next round and must wait another two hours outside in the rain before the second class you entered starts, three hours later than advertised in the schedule.

'Someone else's father will have raised the height.'

In the summer, things can be a bit better, as most outdoor shows have several rings for different classes and the waiting need not be quite as long.

<u>Early days —</u>
<u>parents' guide</u>

1. Never take your children to watch Burghley or Badminton — they may start getting ideas which will eventually bankrupt you.
2. With luck and careful selection the first pony will be a monster and put your child off for life.
3. If the child is still keen, become the heavy parent and give them a hard time when they fail to win the sack race — it could put them off.
4. You will have to do most of the looking after the pony.
5. Your child will be sent home from Pony Club Camp for smoking dope during a teeny orgy in the hay barn — the child constitutes a fire risk.
6. You will have to learn the intricacies of reversing with a trailer or driving a lorry.
7. Your time at shows will be spent putting up practice fences.
8. You will have to go hunting on foot and provide sandwiches.

Cross-country If you're going to be an eventer, this is the bit you've got to enjoy. Happily there are competitions which only involve this element, without boring dressage and technical show jumping. These are:

Hunter trials There are classes to suit every level, and for the youngest competitors there are occasionally contests where you can be led over the tiny jumps by a gasping parent.

Horse trials Now is the time to put all three together and

enter a Pony Club event. This is when the dreams of bigger
things start rattling round the brain. Some of the best Pony
Club cross-country courses have mini replicas of the
famous fences at the 'Big Events'.

If all continues to go well, ambitions to go 'grown-up'
eventing begin to emerge. At novice level, an adult course
differs little from Pony Club, and there is a chance to
compete against, and be beaten by, one of the big names
on one of their younger horses.

Unfortunately, it is probably the time to invest in a new
steed. The ponies have served you well, but now you will
need a horse, and for the first time, ride with Sixteen Hands
Between Your Legs.

One lady owner

To find the right horse you will need expert help, since we
are now entering the realms of expensive purchases. Where
do you start?

The bible of the horse world is the weekly publication
Horse and Hound, which covers every aspect of
equestrianism in its editorial pages, but is read as much for
its extensive classified advertisements – a sort of 'exchange
and cart' and there are several specialist magazines such as
Eventing.

Sit down with your expert, trainer, mother and see what's
on offer. But beware. A typical ad. could read like this,

POTENTIAL THREE-DAY EVENT HORSE,
16hh, 5 year old bay gelding by Old Sod, lightly hunted, good
mover, not a novice ride, genuine reason for sale.
Tel: Wandsworth Common (01) 672 0437 – no time wasters.

This all sounds very good. No price is mentioned, but it's
worth a 'phone call. What is a 'time waster'? You are a 'time

'Lightly hunted.'

waster' because you are not going to buy the horse. You 'phone and discover the price is within your budget, so you make an appointment to see it. You are now in danger of becoming a 'serious time waster' – your own time as well as the vendor's. You have failed to read between the lines of the advertisement and have not done sufficient research. Your potential Badminton winner's sire, Old Sod, wasn't given that name for any old reason. 'Lightly hunted' means that its owners took it out once, when it proved to be such a 'good mover' that it carted its 'novice rider', overtook the Master, hounds and fox, and was sent home in disgrace. In such circumstances there was 'a genuine reason for sale'.

Further enquiries would reveal that Wandsworth Common was not some rural riding haven, but a borough of South-West London.

This 'phoning and viewing ritual can go on for months and you are likely to become a 'professional time waster'.

Even if you think you might at last have found the required horse, tried it over some jumps, ridden it in figures of eight with its nose in the right place and checked its past form and parentage, your expert will adopt the usual purchaser's ploy of running their hands down the back of the beast's front legs. They will then shake their heads with a glum expression. Your heart sinks – the indication being that your Pegasus will break a front axle the first time you ask it to jump a six-inch beanpole. FOLLOW THE RULES:

Rule 1 Don't argue with your expert, just look concerned. There may be nothing wrong with the horse, but you might be able to drop the price by suggesting the horse has an 'if'.

Rule 2 Adopt the 'don't ring us, we'll ring you' principle. You then send your own vet to look the horse over. He unfortunately will discover a hundred things wrong with it. This professional judgement can do two things – put you off the purchase altogether, or reduce the price to the extent that it might be a bargain.

Rule 3 There is no such thing as a bargain.

Rule 4 For professional reasons, a vet is bound to be pernickety. Does his damning report really mean the horse is going to fall to pieces the second you get him home? Almost certainly not. Just remember what happens when you take your car for a service – same headshaking from the mechanic, and an astronomical estimate for a car which has been running perfectly well. Same story if you go for a routine medical and the doctor advises that you should drink only two glasses of wine a week.

The vet, mechanic and doctor have science on their side, but that certainly doesn't mean that the condemned vehicle can't transport the condemned horse, to be ridden by the condemned jockey, to the heights of equestrian achievement.

Rule 5 It's always a risk.

Let's now assume you have taken the risk, bought the horse, at a reduced price, patched him up, and decided that it was all worthwhile. Well done – you are in a minority.

Another way to find your star performer is on a more personal level, but again with the help of your expert, who is likely to know people 'in the business' and hear of suitable horses on the market – whether it's through a dealer or just from another competitor. At the end of the day, all horses are on the market, depending on the price that you are willing to pay. If you have just started eventing, however, and by chance have also just won the pools, don't be tempted to buy last year's Badminton winner – it will end in tears. Ideally, you need a horse just a bit better than you. If the horse is doing it right, you have more chance of looking right. Also, having experienced how to do it courtesy of the horse, you might even start doing it right yourself.

A completely novice horse ridden by a completely novice rider is likely to induce the same disastrous results as two virgins doing it for the first time – especially if the experience has come late in life for both of them.

Historically, horse dealers have the same reputation as second-hand car dealers. Bear this in mind – a carefully-driven Skoda could easily be a better buy than a Roller with a rather dodgy history. The slight advantage of these more private deals in the horse world is that if you are sold a complete 'Friday' horse, word will get around and the vendor's 'trust' will come into question.

You can always take a big risk and go to a Horse Sale: an

Auction. This system works extremely well in racing, but is full of pitfalls for eventers.

It works in racing for several reasons: The big money flat racing horses are sold on their parentage as yearlings, when no one has even sat on them. Once they have raced, they are sold on their form (and of course soundness) – but *jockeys* are hired assassins, and an owner or trainer can hire and fire the rider on a whim. *Eventers* have to work with their mounts to achieve a rapport for much longer than jockeys, who may gallop or jump a potential ride a few times before a race (and quite often never). When buying a racehorse at a sale, the jockey is irrelevant – for an eventer, knowing the horse is more important. At an auction, there is no way to try out the potential purchase. (In eventing the rider gets the glory, in racing the horse – Lucinda has won Badminton, Red Rum has won the Grand National.)

Buying a horse	
	1. Everything you heard about horse dealers is true.
	2. If you sell a horse it will do better with the next owners, who unlike you will make a profit when they sell it.
	3. If you buy a horse that has achieved a great deal, you will achieve considerably less.
	4. A horse with 'spirit' might compete well, but will try and kill you in the stable.
	5. Your purchase is second hand.
	6. Your vet will give it a clean bill of health and look forward to sending you a stream of future bills.
	7. That one little 'if' about the horse on which you decided to take a risk manifests itself immediately.
	8. You will have been 'done'.

5. Debs, nobs and grooms' tricks

You have now spent six months with your new machine, and all is going well. Whichever way you bought it, for some miraculous reason it keeps its nose in doing dressage, doesn't gratuitously knock over the show jumps and shows no aversion to ditches and drops on the cross-country course.

Every evening you (or your groom) walk proudly into the tack room to clean the mud off the saddles, bridles, girths, bits and bobs, and see yet more rosettes pinned up above the sink.

It is now time to reach higher. Apply for a chance to ride in a National Junior Team Trial. Your mother will write the letter for you. (Don't give up the idea of being an eventer if you think you are too old – these 'juniors' can be put in their place further up the ladder.)

She shouldn't write it this way, but probably will.

'To the Chairman of the Junior Selection Committee:

Dear Sir,

My daughter Rosabell learned to ride when she was three. My husband retired from the 19th/28th Uniforms a few years ago, and is now Chairman of the Grouse Conservancy Grousing Committee. In his time, he was a Master of the Staff College Drag Hunt (wasn't everybody?); rode in point-to-points (military races only); and helps with the local Pony Club. Perhaps you will remember his commanding officer, 'Wobbly' Wylye? Anyway, Rosabell is now 15, and has a lovely horse, Hubert, who has been the complete star of the local Pony Club event team. Everyone says that Rosabell will go far and, having seen her dash round the course at the West Ripperton horse trials, where she came fourth (in the individual senior section), I think she could be a candidate for your squad.

My husband, who doesn't know I've written this letter, works in the City now and could support Rosabell for as long as it takes to reach the top. Please give us a place at one of your trials.

Yours most sincerely . . .'

Here is another letter NOT to write:

'Dear Sir,

My daughter is a very talented rider. We run a dairy herd, and her ponies have always been set off against

the farm. We know she is good, but we can't really
afford to continue supporting her unless we find some
sort of sponsorship. She hero-worships the stars, and
we would love her to compete in an event where she
could possibly beat them, as I'm sure she could.
Perhaps just being allowed to enter at the trial would let
you see how good she is. Then someone might help
us to achieve our ambition.

Yours begging . . .'

Don't try either of these approaches.
   Your best bet is to write:

'Dear Sir,

Horse has done it. Rider can. See us at Ripperton.
If daughter blows it, it's her fault.

Horse: Worth a Try
Rider: Aida Chance'

(just add name underneath)

or:

'Dear Bill,

Such fun being on the selection panel with you all
those years ago. Would you believe it, but our son
Michael is now riding the son of the mare I rode round
Burghley in 1970? Should go well. Give them a try.

Love you still,

Binky.'

If you suddenly find that the letter has worked, the invitation to compete in a Trial will mean even more training to make sure that the glowing appraisals don't make you look a fool.

You may be lucky and not come from a totally horsey family. If so, you will have to withstand the ridicule of your non-horsey friends, who won't understand why you can't see them next weekend – because you are going to a show to 'practise'.

At the younger level, this is where many boys drop out. For some reason riding seems a 'cissy' thing to do. But a word of encouragement to boys – you don't need to have posters of 'My Favourite Pony' Blu-Tacked on your bedroom wall to enjoy riding. At the top level it is one of the most demanding and, in a controlled way, risky sports that exist. At a young age, there are probably more girls who sit on ponies, but sports like racing and polo are dominated by men. Even show jumping has more male stars than female – riding is not 'weedy'.

Eventing, however, does have in its ranks many more women than men. Once girls were allowed to do the sport, they took advantage of the longer training hours at their disposal.

If you have got this far with a sound horse, it's time to go off and learn about the animal you are riding. You now go to stay with your trainer, or a 'maestro' of their recommendation.

Here at last you will find people heading for the same goal (not gaol). The great advantage at an 'establishment' is that you will meet people who know all the terminology, and you will learn the names to drop.

Play cool. Sit back and pretend you know all the names, nod every so often, and don't speak until the time is right to drop in a line: 'Yes, but when my grandfather jumped Becher's, he felt that the risk of going on the inside was too much'. It's best really just to listen to everyone else, because this is where you can pick up 'cred' jargon.

It's useful, however, to brush up on the names of some of the foreign international riders and refer to them by Christian name.

You are about to become a fully-fledged eventer. To compete in official trials, you will have to register your horse, and yourself, with the ruling body for a fee, and will be sent a schedule of events for the coming season. The spring and autumn seasons now pretty well merge, but there is a break between October and March. This isn't really a holiday because you will be taking your latest purchase (your second horse) to the dreaded indoor shows.

Horses have this terrible tendency to fall to pieces – even if yours was given a clean bill of health from the vet when you bought him. If you are going to be 'a serious eventer' you will need at least two nags.

All this is going to cost a load of money. The old trailer, towed behind the car, just won't do. You will need a flashy lorry with an elaborate paint job, which will set you back more than the horses it has to carry. The lorry will have to include 'living accommodation', incorporating a shower, cooker, TV set, stereo and fridge. You don't stay in this – you stay at a four-star local hostelry, but you must keep your slave (groom) happy.

In some cases you must even pay your groom. Added to this, you will have to cough up for shoeing the horse, feeding it, lessons with your expensive trainer (who ideally has a middle-European-sounding name), extortionate veterinary bills, and a tack room with Gucci saddles to fit each horse for each phase of the competition.

Almost none of the flash paraphernalia is essential, but if you want to be taken *seriously*, you can't do without it.

6. 'Fortune favours the brave' — and the brave need a fortune

Now comes the tricky bit. To be an eventer you must give up any hope of holding down a job. So how on earth do you pay for it? 'Ah,' you say, 'I'm going to be so good that I can live off the prize money' — Wrong.

They say the appeal of eventing is its healthy amateur image. Put another way, it means the prize money is piss-poor, considering the outlay.

There are several options to this dilemma.

1. Inherit a fortune and give up work.
2. Be spoiled rotten by a parent and never go to work.
3. Do it on a shoestring and take in laundry (not worth the bother).

4. Take up part-time armed robbery or
5. GET SPONSORED.

If you get sponsored you have achieved ultimate 'cred'.
It's a bizarre paradox that the 'amateur character' of the
sport is now attracting commercial concerns, who will
probably one day destroy what they like so much.

WHAT CAN A SPONSOR DO FOR YOU?   Ideally, pay
for everything: lease your horses from you for a large fee;
buy your nine-ton lorry; pay you a retainer; let you keep the
paltry prize money; promise never to 'phone you and
generally indulge you in the fantasy that you will win
Badminton.

At the other end of the scale, your local garage might
offer to help pay for your horse's feed for one year.
WHAT DO YOU HAVE TO DO FOR YOUR SPONSOR?

1. Have his name painted in large letters on both sides of
   the lorry he paid for. (If you haven't been sponsored,
   make up a fake name and spray it on your truck
   regardless – it will help the image.)
2. Wear 'team' anoraks at all events, emblazoned with
   your benefactor's logo (see clothes chapter) and
   coerce your groupies to do likewise.
3. Talk calmly on the 'phone to him when he has rung
   for the fifth time that day.
4. Meet him and his 'guests' at any event where he is
   doing a hospitality number.
5. Take your horse to open his supermarket the day
   before a major competition.
6. Go to trials you didn't want to because his American
   boss is over.

and lastly,

7. Win every time.

To be sponsored	1. The company you write to will have never heard of the sport.
	2. They will have never heard of you.
	3. They will wonder why your sport is one of the most expensive ever devised.
	4. What's in it for them? (Describe in not more than 100 words and send off three wrappers.)
	5. Bow to the dubious taste of your sponsor when it comes to choosing your 'colours'.
	6. Always win (if in doubt, go back to sack races to achieve this – your sponsor wants results).
	7. You will have to introduce your sponsor's wife to your mother. (Only one of them will have something in common.)
	8. The money is never enough.

The commercial interest in the sport has undoubtedly come about because of its 'upmarket' image. Some years ago, 'upmarket' meant understated. Now it's 'FASH to be BRASH and show your CASH'. Ironically, the first advertising hoarding, disguised as a horse box, was used by Gloucestershire's most upmarket eventing double-act. A trend was started, and any horse trial box park now looks like Dover docks during a ferry strike.

How do you get a sponsor? Well, to be honest, you probably won't. (Time to fish out the balaclava and pay a visit to the local Nat West.)

But if you insist on going legit, write another eulogistic letter, photocopy it two hundred times and send copies to anyone who might be a soft touch. This letter should differ from the Junior blurb. Here are some words which *must* be included: **Winner** of . . .; aiming for **Olympics**; riding at

Badminton (don't mention when); string of **top class** horses; like **speaking** at supermarket openings; **please**; you have possibly seen me on *TV*; your **company** and our **sport** have great **links** (eg, you make dog food out of horse meat); this sponsorship will be good for **you**; I need £*X,000*; yours **sincerely**.'

Think positive, you never know what might happen.

Where there's muck there's brass

If all else fails, you could support your eventing indulgences by 'running a yard' and giving lessons. This means renting a block of 'loose boxes' – a row of stables. Here you can keep your own horses and look after half a dozen other peoples'. You will get up at six o'clock every morning, muck out and feed your charges, then after a lukewarm cup of coffee, have to ride them all. Your social life will be non-existent for two reasons:

1. You will be completely knackered
2. You will smell

If you are always knackered and smell anyway, this could be your sport. But to succeed, especially in these conditions, you have to be DEDICATED. (Well, at least pretend to be.)

The most genuinely 'dedicated' event riders are the ones who have never made it. 'I haven't got time for a relationship until I've completed Badminton.' Don't even consider this approach. Have as many 'relationships' as you want, and if you ever get to Badminton you will find there are many more waiting for you there.

Assuming that you have worked out how to pay for your eventing career, you now have to go and do it. And you have to start at the bottom.

Qualifications for the major trials work on a points basis.

**The one-day
events**

1. You will have to get up very early.
2. Your dressage test will be at 9:00 am, the show jumping will be at 12:30, and your cross-country at 5:45.
3. If you are riding more than one horse, you will alternate your clothing at least six times during the day.
4. The dressage arena will be miles away from the horse box park, but next to the cross-country course, where your horse will inevitably be distracted.
5. You will ride faster than you would think prudent just to gain an extra qualification point to get you further up the ladder.
6. Your horse will be lame the next day.
7. The prize money won't have paid for your diesel.
8. For all your heroics, there was no 'public' to witness it. Only a misspelled reference in a local paper you will never see.

Your rise to the top would go something like this:

1. Enter novice event; get round with several minor mishaps.
2. Enter next novice event and clear every jump in both show jumping and cross-country. Unfortunately, you had the worst dressage score.
3. The expensive dressage lessons have paid off, and you are in the minor placings; your horse has gained a qualifying point!
4. You win a novice event, collect points, roll the dice, buy Mayfair and move on.
5. Your horse has now been placed enough to have

become an 'Intermediate'. Bigger jumps, longer courses. He continues to do well, and with the help of your expensive vet, is still in one piece.

6. Now it is time to leave the safety of a one-day event and become a three-day eventer. Roads and tracks, a steeplechase course, and all that jazz.

7. You enjoyed the three-day event, were in the minor placings, gained some more points, and your horse is now categorised as 'Advanced'.

8. The first Advanced one-day event. You are about the only person in your section who hasn't appeared on a television quiz show. You will probably come last, but in such great company. You have almost arrived.

9. You have now got to the stage where you feel confident to enter Badminton.

7. 'Because it was there' (Lord Hunt)

At long last, both you and your horse have qualified for Badminton and the dream is about to become a reality. You have performed more than satisfactorily at some smaller three-day events, and even had a clear round at Burghley, the major autumn Trial.

Burghley is testing enough, but Badminton is in a class of its own.

All those years of going to watch, walking the course and deciding how you would jump to obstacles in the safe knowledge that you are not going to have to, come to a sudden end about ten days before the trial, when a large manilla envelope drops through your letterbox.

In it is your cardboard competitor's badge, your

competitor's car sticker (which under no circumstances should you remove from your windscreen for six months), and most importantly, the running order.

Since there will be as many as eighty entries, the dressage section is spread over two days. This produces misleading posters for those not in the know: **Badminton Three-Day Event – 4th, 5th, 6th, 7th May**.

It doesn't really matter whether you are drawn to do your dressage test on either the Thursday or Friday, and you won't be the first to go, whatever happens. This unenviable slot will be filled by one of the smart Alecs who have got two horses entered. It is quite helpful to be drawn just after someone who you know is appalling at dressage, but a total disaster if you come after one of the established stars, who will get a better mark than they deserve and also make your contribution look like a load of rubbish.

'One thing was certain, it was going to be no picnic'
(Rocky Horror Show)

All your planning, training, and build-up competitions have gone fine, and at last you put the key into the ignition of your lorry, and set off down the M4 to Gloucestershire.

It is possible to go to one-day events all by yourself, but at a three-day, you must have 'help'. If you don't have a full-time groom (silly you), you must borrow one, and your family can be dragged in: to drive your car down, book restaurants, clean your boots, and generally be of support when disaster strikes.

You should probably arrange to arrive some time on Tuesday afternoon and give yourself time to settle in. You begin to see all the background to the event which you will have missed as 'one of the public'. The 250,000 who attend the event haven't really come to see you, but their heroes.

'... for each rider there are 3,125 spectators.'

Nevertheless, if you break this number down, for each rider there are 3,125 spectators. Think of this as your fan club.

The majority of horses are stabled in the smart rectangular stable block beside Badminton House, but the overspills fill several small yards along a private road leading to the park.

Once you have arrived and settled in, it's always nice to go for a leisurely ride in the park. As you go in through the main gates, your first sight will be an enormous canvas village which has sprung up during the past fortnight. Here are the numerous trade stands which will open for business the next day.

In the distance you will see some of the formidable obstacles which await you on Saturday. You are not allowed to show these to your horse, on penalty of being sent home in disgrace. However, your horse probably doesn't want to see them any more than you do.

Many riders now sleep in their luxury trucks. These are parked in an exclusive little field opposite the village shop, and some way away from the vast caravan park designated for the keen paying public, who come for all four days. An enormous amount of people, both riders and public, bring no less than three dogs, so both areas are potential minefields of unwelcome messages, which if trodden into your caravan or lorry carpet will completely spoil your week. A staggering amount of mongrels are also conceived during Badminton week.

Unless you are a dedicated camper, you should only bring drink with you. You don't want to be fiddling with tin openers, powdered mashed potato and burned bacon in your sleeping quarters. Eat out. There are lots of local places eagerly awaiting your custom. (It is however sensible to book somewhere for Saturday night.)

The official start to the competition is the competitors' briefing in the Village Hall. Each rider will be given a map of the course and the programme which includes line drawings of all the cross-country jumps. After this short formality, a convoy of four-wheel drive vehicles sets off on a guided tour of the roads and tracks phase. The route seldom differs and is easy to follow, with yellow directional arrows showing you the way, and the kilometre markers to help you gauge your timing, obviously displayed.

This drive round is lighthearted and you will have later opportunities to go round by yourself. Having taken in a quick walk of the steeplechase course and the second section of roads and tracks, the convoy arrives at the start of the cross-country course. Now for the first time you are allowed to inspect the horrors of Saturday.

The track at Badminton is now fairly established, but

traditionally swaps direction each year. Unlike the Grand National, where the obstacles remain the same, at Badminton subtle differences are introduced to the feature fences, and completely new conundrums are invented annually.

The geography of the park means that an old hand knows what sort of jumps to expect in various places, but the technical nuances need to be worked out in at least three detailed walks round the course.

The course For the sake of argument in your first year the track takes the anti-clockwise route. Fence 1 will be nice and easy – probably beer barrels; two rows on the ground, with one row on top. You then go in front of Badminton House, and again Fence 2 will be easy enough – perhaps a fallen tree. The course then turns right, where a large ditch separates the two fields. The course designer can make what he will of this, but being early on, will (if you're lucky), make it a 'flying' Fence 3, with a racing-type jump in front of the ditch. You then go round the back of the house and meet the first complicated jump, 4. This is known in the trade as an 'island' fence – there are no natural hazards like slopes and ditches, so the designer can put up what he wants, and it will inevitably require you to leave the ground more than once to get out of his 'designer' maze.

There is then another ditch to cross, where there may be solid timber poles above it, 5. Following that, you leave the park by jumping a hedge into a road (Luckington Lane), which will have been covered in peat and closed to traffic, and jump another hedge into the next door farm, 6 and 7. You may then have to jump a couple of walls into and out of the farmyard, 8 and 9. Next are two racing-type fences, but only a few yards apart, one with a ditch on the take-off side, and one on the landing, 10 and 11.

You then turn left and jump back over the road and over

an artificial bank before meeting another ditch. Again, the designer can do what he likes with it, 12. The ditch is wide and smelly, so you are advised not to fall off. You turn right, go alongside the ditch, right again and over another jump, which may include several options for clearing the dyke, 13. You ride along with the ditch on your left, turn left and jump it again, 14, but again, a simple hole in the ground will have been transformed into a seemingly-impossible leap.

Left again and over another artificial bank, 15. Right over the same ditch, 16, you jumped at 3, which again will have been tampered with, to make it more complicated, and you are back in the main park. There is now quite a gap between jumps, because the boggy ground would make them impossible; under some trees, and you may then be invited to jump a brewer's dray, 17. Then onto the TV fence: the lake. Here you may have a choice of jumping a log or upturned punt and dropping into the pond, 18, perhaps taking in an additional bank in the middle and leaving the water over a boat house or wood-fronted bank, 19.

Turning right, you meet yet another artificial bank, where you are required to leap on, over a ditch, sit for one stride, jump a timber pole and drop considerably before landing, 20.

Soon a sharp left and a very steep downhill bank, where again the designer can let his imagination run riot, 21, right, up another bank with a jump at the top, 22, and another soggy bit of ground until you reach a part of the park where a long-lost village used to exist. The old road has been excavated for the jump, so you will have to leap an obstacle, with a sharp downhill landing side, drop onto a 'road', jump up out of it again and jump something else on your way out, 23. There is then a long stretch of no jumps, when you clatter over one of the park roads and reach an old quarry, 24, where you will have several options how to jump down into it. Then up a steep bank with a wall at the top, 25.

A short canter on flat ground to another island fence, 26, before another big ditch, 27. A sharp left turn and you jump into a small copse, 28. You may then have another artificial fence, 29, before jumping out of the copse, 30. Turn right, jump a fairly simple fence back into the park, 31, back over the road, hang a bit left and the last fence is in sight. For several years this has had the added complication of having a roof over it! Then it is back down the chute as you go through the finish flags.

'You cannot be serious' (John McEnroe)

Having done your first walk round the course and had lunch, you must now start preparing for the nerve-jangling experience of the first horse inspection. In recent years, this has become quite a thing with the spectators, and happens in the grandiose setting right in front of Badminton House. At this stage, you rather hope and assume that your horse will pass the inspection, which requires you, or your groom, to lead it at the trot in front of a panel of bowler-hatted officials. They will confer with one another, shake their heads diligently, and if you are lucky, will give the thumbs-up sign to the commentator, 'Number 41, Pass'.

If your dressage test isn't till Friday, you can now go off and get pissed, since all you will have to do the next day is walk the course again and take your horse up to the practice dressage arenas. These you will have to share with other riders, and do some last-minute wiggles and circles in the hope that it will all go all right tomorrow. With luck, your foreign-sounding trainer will also be on hand to offer instructions such as 'a bit more lower leg', 'now lengthen', 'bend more to the left'. These bizarre commands are not telling you to grow six inches and lean over, but for you to squeeze your calf into the horse's side (or give it a bloody great kick if the trainer can't see), and try to get the horse to lengthen its stride. You will have learned all this jargon during the hundreds of boring dressage lessons that you will have had over the years. These have brought you to this hallowed turf. Unfortunately, however much your trainer has ridden your horse at home (to bully some sense into it), rules state that at a competition you've got to do it yourself. Even your groom, who is more than likely a better rider than you, is only allowed to ride the beast 'on a loose rein'.

On Thursday evening, there is a drinks party in Badminton House for riders, owners and officials, which is always absolutely packed. Rows of cars pull up outside the house, and you enter through the main door and pass through a vast hall, where the shuttlecock game was reputedly invented. Because there are so many people, it is essential to make friends with one of the waitresses very quickly. If possible, take up a permanent position by a door – anyone you want to talk to will undoubtedly pass by at some time, but much more importantly, your glass should never find itself empty. The conversation will be boring, as the only thing anyone talks about at this stage is how they are going to jump such-and-such a fence on Saturday, with the usual concerned mutterings, even from the stars, that the course is the most difficult ever. If this is your first time, you don't need to hear things like this. During your more detailed walk round that afternoon, when you will have carefully paced out the distances between the elements, you don't want to hear that 'only an idiot' would go your route. If you are sensible, an expert or old sweat will have walked with you, so these dangers can be minimised. Nevertheless, it's another good excuse to ignore technical conversations and settle down to the more important task of (a) getting pissed again (even if your dressage *is* the next day) and (b) arranging to go out to dinner with a bunch of friends to continue the process.

On Friday morning you will wake up with a God-awful hangover, and come to the conclusion that you don't really want to do a dressage test in two hours' time. Well, you've got to. While your horse is being tarted up, you try the same process with yourself, with disappointing results. You put on all your finery and make your way to the stables.

'You climb on board your horse and instantly feel dizzy.'

You climb on board your horse and instantly feel dizzy. You take a deep breath and ride back into the park, back to the practice arenas, where today all the other frantically-circling riders will also have made an attempt to dress perfectly.

At this level of competition, the tests last about ten minutes, so, about two horses before you, you move into the collecting enclosure and keep trotting about till it's your turn. You feel quite calm, because, surprisingly, your horse has been going well in practice, but suddenly you are in the large area surrounded by tented grandstands, fluttering national flags and the realisation that in less than one minute you will actually be *COMPETING at Badminton*. You will seize up, and transmit, by telepathy, your nerves to the horse, who has started to have some of his own. At Badminton you will have three judges at the far end, not now in cars, but in special judging boxes. A bell will sound and in you go.

You should know the order of the movements without even thinking by now, but your mind is still likely to go blank. Relax by humming to yourself or remembering the filthiest joke you know. Try not to come out with the punchline or chorus in hearing range of the judges, as using your voice whilst riding the test is penalised. It's also useful to have developed ventriloquist's skills so that you can converse with your horse, 'For Christ's sake woahh you bugger,' while maintaining a fixed grin.

Eventually the agony is over. It hasn't gone as badly as you thought. Not the shaming embarrassment of the bronco display which you feared. The crowd has been politely silent during your efforts, and equally politely ripple to applause as you leave the arena on a long rein. At which stage, your horse bucks, nearly throws you, and breaks into a canter as you fumble to regain control.

After this ordeal you can relax as you go for a final pipe-opening gallop, after hearing your dressage score announced, then put the horse away before your final walk round the course.

By this third walk round, everyone will tell you that the fences start to look a bit smaller and more manageable.

'Woah you bugger.'

Don't believe them. On the other hand, don't dwell at them at all on this last trip, you should have worked out which routes to take by now, and any last-minute doubts will only make matters worse.

Tomorrow is going to be the most exciting and nerve-racking day of your eventing career. This is what you have been building up to for all these years. There is no point in being a goody-two-shoes and going to bed early – YOU WILL NOT SLEEP. Every jump will run through your brain, and any amount of trying to count sheep jumping them won't help at all. It is much more important to keep up the routine you have been adopting all week – get pissed.

However you feel in the morning, you will still wake up much earlier than you wanted to. Don't try and stay in bed, those jumps will start flashing through your subconscious again. The combined effects of the night before, and a colony of butterflies whizzing about your stomach will kill any thoughts of breakfast. You are not due to ride till mid-afternoon and there is far too much time to kill.

Go to the village shop and buy every newspaper, even the 'grown-up' ones which you would never read at home.

Some people even go and walk the course yet again, but this is more likely to increase nerves, not allay them.

You will have been issued with timesheets telling you exactly when you should start and finish each phase, so once the brain is up to it, you start working out when you aim to pass the kilometre guides on the roads and tracks. These you write down on a postcard or large square of sticking plaster to wear on your sleeve.

When the early competitors start to go, make your way to the start and finish enclosure, which is open only to riders and immediate connections. Here there will be an area set aside with a few closed-circuit TV sets, and, sitting on the ground, or craning to see, will be other later riders and the connections of the couple of riders currently doing their thing on the course.

All the screens show the same picture, which is at the whim of the TV director. If a star is on the course, and also your best friend, you will not see your best friend. You may also not see the star either, as TV directors seem to love cutting to crowd shots or ducks on the lake, just as something you wanted to see comes onto the screen.

At least by watching the early riders you will get an idea whether the course designer really has gone mad, or whether there is an outside chance that you might get round.

You then make your way back through an unbelievable mass of humanity to change into your gladiatorial kit, take your saddle to the start of Phase A, officially weigh out, and await your horse.

Everything is in place, you are legged into the saddle, the countdown begins, and away you go – just a couple of hundred yards through bustling crowds, through a park gate and into the uncanny quiet of the first roads and tracks section. Here you can actually relax, and dedicated athlete that you are, can even pull out a packet of fags and light up. You might occasionally come across a couple of lost spectators who will spend the rest of the afternoon trying to find their way back to the park and will miss all the action – there is advice for spectators later.

After about twelve minutes, you will arrive at the steeplechase course, wait for a short time and again be sent on your way. Provided you don't have an unexpected disaster, this bit is quite easy and quite fun. Both you and the horse are getting into the idea of jumping, and your blood is no longer at freezing temperature. After you have completed this section, you can let your horse walk for a short time while you get out the packet of fags again. One or two incredibly keen riders dismount their horses (within the rules provided you are back in the saddle when you complete the phase) and run alongside. DON'T DO THIS – you haven't spent all this time getting your horse fit enough to carry you round only to run alongside it. The last stretch of this second roads and tracks section takes you down a wide undulating avenue back towards the park. At the top end is a tall lodge building where a previous Duke of Beaufort installed a mistress, to whom he would canter up the avenue and see, then return the way you're going to the house.

For the superstitious, there always seem to be single magpies down this stretch. The nerves aren't helped by the increasing sound of the cross-country loudspeakers as you get nearer and nearer.

Suddenly you are back in the park again, and have to find your way through the throng to the nerve-centre 'box', where another team of bowler hats will check if your horse is fit enough to continue. You then have the compulsory ten-minute break; an increasingly-important visit to the loo; another look at the TV monitors; and all too soon you are waiting for the countdown for your date with destiny. Try to avoid picking your nose or scratching your bum at this moment, as more than likely the TV director will have you in close up.

'Try to avoid picking your nose.'

The course will now look completely different to how it did when you walked round. You won't get lost, because throughout your whole ride you will be riding through a gauntlet of people up to ten deep as you approach each jump. You just have to go into a private bubble and get on with the job.

This bubble can easily be broken, especially if you have the misfortune to part company from your horse. Other hazards can be equally distracting. Although all spectators are warned (on pain of death) to keep their dogs on leads, one or two hounds are bound to get loose, and sod's law dictates this will happen when you are on the course.

If a miscreant pooch has found itself on your approach line to a jump, you will be tempted to shout in no uncertain terms for the animal to be removed. ON NO ACCOUNT DO THIS. One dog in the way has a good chance of being avoided, fifty people leaping forward to retrieve it will cause serious problems.

Things continue to go well. You have been sensible and taken all the easy options and you are clear coming up to the lake. Here there will be about four thousand people waiting to be entertained. By that they mean they want you to get a ducking. Try not to play to the gallery.

It suddenly dawns on you that you may well get round, but do keep concentrating to the last jump – you wouldn't be the first person to fall there. Then 'Allelujah', you are through the finish flags and cantering up the chute. You dismount, weigh in, and can't believe that it's happened. A TV man may then thrust a microphone up your nose and ask you what you felt of your ride. Your reply will be gibberish, but your breathlessness gives it credence.

You haven't had a cigarette for a quarter of an hour, so you instantly light up after your interviews. The horse will be taken away by your helpers to be washed down and pampered, and you go back into the TV area to watch the last riders go. You then go off to *get pissed*.

The stable area on the Saturday night is a hive of activity, with horses having their legs hosed with cold water, and all

'Try not to play to the gallery.'

types of embrocation will be rubbed on to ensure your
mount is sound for the final day. Remember, this is the big
snag with three-day eventing – you have done all the
heroics and come through with flying colours, but it's not
yet over.

When you go to sleep on Saturday night your mind will
yet again flash images of every jump on the course at you –
but this time it is a dream, not a nightmare.

On the Sunday morning you will have to get up earlier
than you would normally wish to, and check that your horse

still has the full complement of legs. You may then take him for a walk around the park before having him tarted up for the final inspection in front of the house.

This last inspection is the most nerve-wracking because even if you think your horse is sound as a bell, the panel may disagree. You might be able to distract the 'bowler hats' by leading up your horse in the nude, but this ploy might just make them suspicious. It would be the final ignominy for your horse to fail, and for you to be arrested before ten o'clock on a Sunday morning.

'You've done it.'

The show jumping phase is run in reverse order of the overnight placings. The lower-placed competitors will probably have to do this in the morning. This will mean you, but is an advantage since almost no one will be watching – and it doesn't really matter how many poles you knock down provided you get through the finish flags. YOU'VE DONE IT!

The rest of the day will be bliss. You can go shopping in the trade stands, have lunch, *get pissed*, get back onto your horse for the afternoon parade and watch in peace as the top riders fight it out for the prizes.

The Big Ones

<u>Minus</u>	
	1. On arriving at Badminton or Burghley you will realise you are out of your depth.
	2. Your 'kiddy' dream is rapidly turning into a nightmare.
	3. You will find that Alka-Seltzer doesn't help you as much as it did at home.
	4. However fit you thought you were, walking the long course three times will seize you up.
	5. You will have an embarrassing (and later embarrassed) fan club.
	6. You will only be on TV if you have a spectacular fall.
	7. Your sponsor will have hired a hospitality marquee but the horse is failed by the panel before the competition starts.
	8. You realise that your groom would have ridden the horse better than you.

Plus

1. What the hell?, You've made it to the big time.
2. You are spending a week full of parties with a large number of friends, which only the riding interrupts.
3. Even if you fall at the first fence, you will always be able to bore your grandchildren about 'When I rode here'.
4. You will have overcome the worry about making a fool of yourself in public — if you do, nothing in your life will ever be worse.
5. If you get round, a rich foreigner will want to buy your horse.
6. You will be noticed by the team selectors — sell immediately.
7. Buy yourself a property —
8. . . . and retire to real life

8. 'Give us a twirl'

(Bruce Forsyth)

If horses, lorries, blacksmiths, stables, vets, feed, grooms, entry fees, registration fees and riding lessons haven't quite broken the bank, you haven't finished there. Eventing probably requires you to buy more clobber for both your horse and yourself than almost any pastime imaginable. Imelda Marcos would probably run a close second to the size of your wardrobe. Why didn't you have an ambition to be a champion swimmer — all you would need is a pair of trunks and a rubber skull cap.

Although Red Indians rode almost naked, with not much more than a piece of string through the horse's mouth for steering, to become a champion eventer you will need a bit more.

For the horse

Basic requirements include a saddle, which not only fits the horse's back, but which fits your back-end also. But all the straps and buckles to keep the saddle on the horse, and you on the saddle, have to be bought separately. You will need a girth, the strap which holds the saddle on, stirrup leathers to attach to either side, and stirrup irons to put your feet in.

You can usually buy a bridle made up of all the straps, buckled in the right place, and including your steering. Unfortunately, to clean it you are supposed to take the thing to bits, and a Chinese puzzle of reassembling can be as difficult as replacing a stripped car engine, for the novice. (This again is where the groom comes in.)

'This again is where the groom comes in.'

As you progress, more sophisticated additions may be needed – a selection of different 'bits' for the horse's mouth, different nosebands to strap the beast's mouth shut, straps to stop the saddle slipping backwards (martingales), spongy or woolly pads for under the saddle (numnahs) and a whole host of other accessories. When you are getting nearer the top of the sport, your horse may require a completely different set of tack for each phase (and remember you will have at least two horses by now).

To stop your valuable animal from hurting its legs you may also require sets of padded guards for them to wear round their lower legs – 'boots'. These you will lose with the regularity of socks at the laundry.

Even in the stable, your horse will have to wear clothes, since you will have clipped off his own insulation. They even make waterproof mackintoshes to keep him dry in the field.

Now for your wardrobe

You will look a complete Wally if you do everyday riding in your immaculate competition clothes. Only people who ride in Hyde Park do this, because they never go to competitions.

Trousers You can ride in just jeans, but your legs are likely to get rubbed and pinched rotten. If you insist on the denim look, wear a pair of leather cowboy 'chaps' over the top, but pass on the rhinestones and tassles. A pair of stretch jodhpurs is ideal because you can wear either long or short boots with them. Ordinary shoes are not to be recommended as your foot could slip through the stirrup and leave you being dragged along like a Western stuntman.

For day-to-day riding your jodhpurs can be any colour,

which hides the dirt, but you will need a pair of buff or white ones for public display. They now make light-coloured breeches with a dark suede seat and inner leg to stop you slipping in the saddle. This may be effective, but it will make you look as if you have had a terrible fright.

Footwear The most standard type of short boot is the elastic-sided leather jodhpur boot, but a more modern equivalent is the ribbed rubber lace-up 'mucker' boot. For general riding, full-length rubber riding boots are quite in order, but after each day of wear your socks will take on a life of their own. They are very 'naff' for competition, however, especially when either worn by children or with a two-inch gap between the top of the boot and your leg. You will eventually need an expensive pair of long leather boots. Again, in top competition, you will need three pairs: slightly longer with a curved top for dressage, perhaps a lightweight pair of racing boots for cross-country and a standard pair for show jumping.

General top wear You will be forced to ride in almost all weathers, so you will need one of the numerous brands of padded waistcoats or anoraks, and a waxed waterproof coat. Unless you fancy blue fingers, gloves are a must, and even on warm days help you grip the reins.

For competition, there are different garments for each phase. In dressage, a double-breasted cutaway tail coat in tasteful black (for Advanced competitions, a white cravat-type tie on a collarless shirt, and a yellow-coloured waistcoat). Real waistcoats can induce serious perspiration during a dressage test, so bogus tabs are usually fitted under the front of the tails with poppers.

On the cross-country phase you can let your individuality come through by choosing your own coloured sweater and helmet cover. These can be as garish as you like. When you consider that two of eventing's best-known stars chose primrose yellow, and purple, as their 'strip', you realise that taste is no prerequisite. Underneath your technicolour dreamcoat you will wear a foam-padded vest which will make you look a stone heavier than you are.

For show jumping you will wear a well-cut riding jacket in either scarlet, black or dark blue, and a black helmet cover.

Hats However few grey cells you might have had in the first place when you started out on your quest to be an eventer, it's advisable to protect them so always wear a hard hat. There are moves to phase out the standard riding hat in favour of ones with harnesses. Apart from the standard jockey helmet for cross-country riding with the detachable peaked 'silks', most of the new innovations look awful, but you have the choice. Apart from the dressage phase, some kind of chinstrap is now compulsory in British competition. For 'top' dressage, however, a 'top' hat completes the tail coat look. It is considered 'correct' for girls to have neat buns, but if you normally fancy the 'gamin' look, you can buy fake buns to pin on.

All your competitive kit should look immaculate, but under no circumstances should it look new. If, when all togged up, you look ANYTHING like the models in riding-wear advertisements, you have got it wrong, and should return to Hyde Park whence you came.

If you reach the dizzy heights of top competition, or even International honours, then you may have another sartorial problem on your hands. Any normal competitor, when not actually engaged in the contest, will wear normal clothes. A sponsored rider, however, will be expected to wear his anorak proclaiming his benefactor's name in most public places. The benefactor will have even worse taste than you.

When it comes to International Championships, the

— *'It is considered correct for girls to have neat buns — BUNS!!'*

situation gets worse. All sorts of sponsors pop up through the woodwork offering garments for the team.

A team uniform is presented; publicity photographs taken and the riders and their manager expected to wear it at all official functions, drinks parties, horse inspections, etc.

The designer will have been given a brief for this 'upmarket country pursuit' and come up with either a 'his and hers' matching tweed ensemble (and nobody 'upmarket' or 'country' would wear matching tweed, let alone his and hers), or 'blazer and slacks/skirts' effect, so that the man looks like a bowls official and the girl like an air hostess.

If you care what you look like, don't get selected for a team.

Clothes for the rider

1. Don't follow equestrian fashion trends.
2. Spend the money on properly made kit, then abuse it, to make it look worn.
3. Never wear anything brand new, it will make you look as if you took up riding yesterday (even if you did).
4. Remove all facial hair (whichever sex) — this will give the same impression.
5. Don't wear earrings (either sex), apparently they can get caught in trees.
6. Affect a look of smiling acceptance when wearing sponsored garb.
7. Don't wear thermals, even on the coldest day — you will start sweating in less than a minute.
8. Use lots of make-up for the dressage (either sex), but none thereafter.
9. It's not done to wear a white shirt and black silk as your colours (British team colours) unless you have earned them.

Part II

9. 'Any which way you can' (Clint Eastwood)

As you will have seen, the sport of horse trials is mind-blowingly complicated and time-consuming. To make it happen at all requires an army of background organisation and personnel to run the competitions for the benefit of the riders.

By now you will have sensibly decided to abandon any ambitions of taking up the sport, but think it would be fun to 'be involved'. Ninety-eight per cent of help is voluntary, but there are one or two jobs which pay a modest fee. The administration would fall apart if every helper demanded money, and eventing plays on the myth that it is an honour to play some minor official role. To this end, there are company directors happily doing shop-floor tasks, and retired generals doing corporals' jobs such as organising car parks.

If you want to get involved in eventing by proxy, there are lots of avenues open to you. Remember, you are joining an 'upmarket country pursuit'.

Since the calendar is so packed, quite a few competitions are held mid-week, so once again it helps if you don't have, or don't need, a proper job. Possession of a bus pass would almost guarantee that you are in the right age group.

Jump judge Every obstacle on the cross-country course needs to be officially monitored, and any refusal or fall of a competitor logged on a score sheet. These sheets will be collected at regular intervals by a small child on an out-of-control pony and taken back to the scorers. Every event has between twenty and thirty jumps, so your first official post will probably be as a jump judge. You will not need to have any prior knowledge, and as such will be in the majority. You will be briefed at the start of the day by a senior official, whose speech is almost certain to muddle you, and issued with whistles, stopwatches and a bunch of flags to wave in case of an emergency. In theory, the first time you will be in charge of a very easy jump which won't cause problems – so it will. You may then get promoted to more complicated obstacles with several elements, until some years later, and completely ga-ga, your services will no longer be required.

You will be able to take your car to the fence and you always need an accomplice – in theory for safety in times of trouble, but more importantly to man the ship while you disappear into the bushes. Bring your own picnic and bar. You may be given a packed lunch, which under no circumstances should be eaten. The budget menu *always* consists of: one paper plate, set of plastic cutlery, two sweating slices of composite ham, a limp piece of lettuce, one tomato, a dollop of coleslaw which smells and tastes

'These sheets will be collected by a small child on an out-of-control pony.'

exactly what it looks like, a dollop of potato salad and a stale bun. You might even get a slice of chemical Black Forest Gateau.

At the end of a long day, your car will get bogged down and the tractor which eventually pulls you out will bend your front axle. In the summer the car will be safe, but you will be bitten to death by mosquitoes, as you have been given the water jump to watch over.

If you really draw the short straw, you might be invited to monitor a compulsory turning flag on the furthest outpost of the roads and tracks at a three-day event. This job is about as interesting as being a professional scarecrow, but you can be secure in the knowledge that 'Your Sport Needs You'.

Things to bring
as a jump judge   1. A tow rope.
    2. A sharp instrument, to either release an
       offending telegraph pole, put the horse
       out of its misery, or see to the rider who
       should have known better.
    3. Something decent to eat and drink.
    4. A comfortable deckchair (or hammock).
    5. A biro that works.
    6. A roll of loo paper for the bushes.
    7. The schedule for Radio 4.
    8. A strong assistant who can personally lift
       a horse out of a ditch (cf Toy Boy).

Dressage judges If you are a fierce-looking mature lady, this is the job for you. General consensus among competitors is that absolutely no equestrian experience is needed to fulfil this important role. All you are required to do is park your car at the correct end of the dressage arena (if in doubt, look to see where the other judges have parked), turn on the heating and radio and sit there for up to five hours. You will be given a 'coffee' break at elevenses, so to keep up the serious image it is suggested that your sloe gin is disguised in a thermos flask.

This seemingly-untaxing job is rather spoiled by the continuous stream of riders entering your arena, doing their little show and at the least expecting you to acknowledge them at the beginning and end of their efforts. If you are hidden behind a copy of the morning paper they may suspect your judgements.

With you in the car will be your 'writer' who is meant to scribble your comments for each movement, and the marks. This procedure can be avoided. While waiting for the next rider, you just make up the marks and comments,

'. . . taking care to notice if one of the competitors is an eventing star.'

Dressage judge — what you need

1. A desperate need for something to do.
2. A low boredom threshold.
3. No experience.
4. A 'writer' who does have experience.
5. A pencil sharpener (always do it in pencil because you can change your mind later).
6. A credible horn on your car.
7. A fast set of wheels to disappear before your victims know their scores.
8. A total belief in your own infallibility.

taking care to notice if one of the competitors is an eventing star. If so, give them an average of 8 out of 10, and if you've never heard of them, between 5 and 6. This system works every time. Riders will never agree with your marks anyway, and at least you haven't exposed your ignorance by putting an Olympic champion bottom of the list.

Commentating If you like the sound of your own voice, volunteer to man the public address system. This is one of the more sought-after posts, and you might even get paid for your services. There are some commentators happy enough to hear themselves on the tannoy without thought of remuneration. DON'T BE ONE OF THEM. There are, however, several stipulations.

If your microphone manner is similar to a stand-up comic in a working mens' club, you need not apply (remember the 'upmarket' etc, etc). You will also need to pick up the jargon, which is nothing more than a string of clichés strung together. Nobody actually listens to a word you're saying, but the background ambience of a 'civilised' voice, and the occasional familiar phrase coming out of the loudspeaker, reassures everyone that all is well.

Your commentating box is the nerve centre of the competition. You and your colleagues actually have a role much more important than your ramblings. All round the course, radio operators will report the whereabouts of a particular horse and request you to send out emergency services when necessary. A colleague will plot each horse's movement on a board in front of you – rather like Wrens pushing model boats around in the operations room scenes of old war movies. Naval command, however, never had radio interference from local mini-cab firms:

'Horse number 25 is clear at fence 14 Woodstock Avenue to go to Heathrow, a Mister Sedgefield fallen at the water jump, we need the vet for a regular customer. Roger

'. . . similar to a stand-up comic . . .'

Charlie five, fifteen minutes taking the long route between the gate and fence 12.'

Commentators are expected to mention the major and minor sponsors during their bulletins, give a bit of background guff about the riders, sound calm when there is a panic going on and MOST importantly, remember to switch off the microphone when not reporting. Joanna's mother does not want to know how you fancy your chances with her nubile daughter, even if for once everyone else is riveted.

This job is fun, so have elocution lessons and learn the clichés: 'Good morning and welcome to the Henry Root Wet Fish Ltd Horse Trials here at Anchovy Hall. Each of the thirty fences has been kindly sponsored by local companies: Fence 1, The Start-Rite Starter; 2, Basil's Brush, sponsored by Basingstoke's best-known chimney sweep, Arthur Basil, 3,' etc . . .

'The first horse to go cross-country will start in just over five minutes, so we would like to remind you to keep your dogs on leads at all times. The course distance is 7,410 metres, with an optimum time of 13 minutes.

'Into the starting box now comes number 1, the reigning Volkswagen under-21, novice, Futurity, never to have been placed on her own horse before, local point winning champion, all the way from Essex, Cruella de Ville riding Morgan Forklift Trucks, Europe, Ltd's Dalmatian Cl.

'They start with a dressage score of 58 and a rather unfortunate show jumping round incurring an expensive 30 penalties, making their total so far 88. And they're off . . .

'And over the Start-Rite Starter as they make their way round this inviting course, designed by Sebastian Chesterfield-Sofa and built by Gavin Plank. We learn that Cruella has parted company from Dalmatian at the Oedipus Complex . . . a combination fence in the woods . . . but they are both on their feet . . . About to start now is the former European champion Meryl Streep riding African Farm. Cruella none the worse for her fall approaches The Famous Grouse (Mrs Bottomley the jump judge) at the David Hockney Bigger Splash at the far end of the course.

'Sadly Meryl and African Farm have fallen at the Clap Trap and Dalmatian has been retired at the Berlin Wall . . . (silence while you discover Meryl is still in a heap and the first-aid is dispatched) . . . And while we have this minor hold-up, I am pleased to be able to inform you of a gala to be performed by the Morris Men from Mitcham here in Anchovy Park on June 21st. Tickets are on sale at the Secretary's Tent . . . Meryl Streep and African Farm have also retired, but the course is now open . . .

'(later) . . . Number 23, Dobbin the Unlikely, is

approaching the penultimate of these thirty fences, and we await her time with interest. Over the last and through the finish and we should be able to give you a provisional score in a few seconds. I hasten to add that all these results are provisional, but with only three time penalties and a total of 35 that puts her into fourth place in Section Z . . .

'(6 hours later) . . . And the last horse on the course, Barn Door and Naomi Knee-Trembler, has completed the course so we would like to remind jump judges to stay in position until their final slips have been collected and once again thanks to . . .'

| <u>To be a</u>
<u>commentator</u> | 1. Cultivate a baritone 'upmarket' voice (whichever sex).
2. Bring along a good supply of newspapers to read when you are 'resting'.
3. Ignore the plastic lunch and go in search of the sponsor's tent.
4. Your voice will sound better the more gins and cigarettes you have during the day, but your grasp of the situation will deteriorate.
5. No one is listening to you, so pass over the responsibility, and pass out.
6. Mention as many sponsors as you can while you are 'on', because they will be worth a free drink when you have come to.
7. Be used to hearing your own voice. There is usually a delay before your words of wisdom hit the tannoy, and it will then echo round the course as you struggle with the second sentence.
8. Make sure you get paid. |

Landowner/organiser To run any kind of horse trials a suitable site must be found, and that means acreage with a benevolent landowner. They may be able to run the Horse of The Year Show at Wembley, but you couldn't exactly have a cross-country course in North London.

Finding a site or checking out one which has been offered is the job of one of the sport's few salaried employees – A Technical Delegate. In theory at least, he is an expert. He may design the course also, or advise the keen amateur who has dreams of turning his farm into another Badminton.

If you fancy your talent at designing a course, don't be too ambitious and come up with lots of 'clever' new ideas. It is perfectly acceptable to borrow ideas from other events,

To be a landowner	
	1. You have failed to make any money out of farming.
	2. A keen young man in moleskin trousers driving a Japanese 4-wheel drive, turns up at your door. He was in the same house as you at school, and you have been flattered by a call from HQ asking if you would 'run an event'.
	3. It seemed a good idea at the time, but you begin to have your doubts when a division of JCB panzers arrive on your estate.
	4. What do you tell the cowman?
	5. Your farm staff resign.
	6. You are left with 1,000 acres of eventing land.
	7. You too are now looking for a sponsor and will have to be polite to non-landowning 'millionaires'.
	8. Go organic.

'A keen young man in moleskin trousers . . .'

and on different land no two jumps will ever be exactly the same. The dimensions of the obstacles for each level are stipulated in the rule book, so with advice you can't go too far wrong – *and* you won't have to carry the can. The Delegate takes some responsibility and the Official Steward on the day takes the ultimate rap. He has the power to make you change anything.

Landowners are beginning to do 'alternative farming' and some may hope to earn something out of holding an event on their site. A highly-efficient intense farm is not the place to run a horse trial, but if you fancy a few star equestrian names galloping over your rolling pastures once a year, invite a Delegate down to look over your allotment.

You may have farmworkers, whom you can spare, to construct your inspirational course, and you may also have all the timber at your disposal, but your best bet is to consult and hire the pros. This will involve considerable capital outlay (everything in eventing does) so you also will need to go in search of a sponsor, not only for the prize money, but to help towards the building costs.

Course builders There are a handful of professional jump constructors. Most of these are personable young men whose *major* academic qualification was an 'O' level in carpentry from a public school (whereas a Technical Delegate's qualification was being a Major). If you are a dab hand with a chainsaw, an artist with a creosote brush, a natural pile driver, and can handle a JCB like a Mini, this could be your calling.

You will need a battered four-wheel drive truck (Japanese or British) and contacts at both British Telecom and British Rail for your supply of telegraph poles and sleepers. Even these items have been known to fall off the back of a lorry.

**Bill and Ben
(course builders)**

1. Lose your accent and start talking rustic.
2. Learn to drive bizarre vehicles.
3. Make knowledgeable remarks about the surrounding wildlife, 'Did you see that woodhen, she was mating there last year.' 'I tried one of those mushrooms and spent two days in intensive care.'
4. Don't worry about what your hands look like.
5. Why should you be digging gratuitous holes in the ground?
6. What the hell, it's someone else's park.
7. And you can erect your wooden sculptures.
8. Your name will be in the programme.

You will also need to know the jargon of the trade: 'revetting a ditch' (shoring it up with sleepers), 'using a godfather' (a lower support pole), and know some of the more common names of standard fences: an Elephant Trap (poles sloping away over a ditch); a Trakhener (a single pole slung over a ditch); a Tiger Trap (Eeyore's house without a roof), etc, etc.

If you can get good enough at fence building you might even become a Technical Delegate yourself one day, and wear a shiny enamel badge despatched from Headquarters.

Event secretary This job is to be avoided at all costs. Your 'phone will never stop ringing for months before the competition. People will enter, then un-enter. Riders will fill in all their forms incorrectly (that is if they can write in the first place). Your electric typewriter will overheat. Your computerised system will 'go down' at a crucial moment, and you will have inherited a job for life.

Secretary/ Organiser	1. Go ex-directory.
	2. Do a bunk with the entry money.
	3. Don't volunteer in the first place.

'The importance of being earnest' (Oscar Wilde)

Grooms You have probably decided already that this is not the job for you – well done. It has one serious disadvantage over any other sorts of involvement in eventing: you actually have to know something about horses. This knowledge can only be achieved by a lifetime's slavery and large doses of that most dreadful ingredient – dedication.

'Because they are small.'

In racing stables, the grooms are called 'lads' and are almost all male. They usually arrive in a yard after they have left school with no horse knowledge whatsoever, but have been packed off by their families because they are small and might one day become jockeys. With all other horse sports in Britain, grooms are almost exclusively girls. This section is for you.

Your route to the top (?) would probably follow this pattern:

While still in single figures, you bicycle to the local stables after school and help clean the tack and sweep the yard. As you get older, you may be trusted with brushing the ponies, filling their waterbuckets and eventually mucking them out. You will be rewarded with an occasional ride on one of the school ponies on the few days when there are less paying customers.

You leave school at the first opportunity and decide on 'a career with horses'. The local stables pay you a few quid pocket money a week.

Most of this hard-earned cash goes on pony magazines and posters. Your bedroom wall at home doesn't have a single picture of a pop star, but all your riding heroes are there. Your parents suggest it's about time you left home, and you apply to a competition yard to become a working pupil (see *passim*). The yard will have a head girl of dubious sexuality who is your immediate boss.

You will stay here for a year and your accommodation will be spartan in the extreme: either an old caravan with a small gas heater, surrounded by dirty Horse of The Year Show coffee cups and a pile of laundry waiting to be washed, or a condemned cottage whose only warmth comes from the Aga on which is always simmering some gruel-like horse feed or kaolin veterinary preparation.

'Above the range will hang an assortment of drying boots . . .'

Above the range will hang an assortment of drying horse boots, bandages and saddle pads, all of whose combined aroma might disguise your own dubious 'musk'.

During the year, you will at least get the chance to go to lots of competitions and become an assistant groom. Unfortunately, however, in the first flush of youth you will almost certainly have to forego any hope of social contact with the opposite sex. This is clever psychology on behalf of 'the system'. You will become emotionally attached to the horses in your care. This means you have achieved Grade 2 Dedication. Part of the deal is that you will also get riding instruction on decent horses from people who might know what they're talking about. At the end of the year, you can take an official exam, put a few letters after your name, and start looking for a real job.

If you have stuck it that long, you probably have masochistic tendencies and enjoy it. It would be a shame to spoil your agony, but your fortunes could now change quite dramatically, if not financially. You will be entering a special clique, and joining the eventing circuit. The work will be just as hard, but 'your' horses and 'your' rider will be representing *you*. In quite a short time, the other grooms (and riders) will know you, and you have every right to bask

Grooms	
	1. Be an animal lover.
	2. Don't get caught.
	3. The horses in your care never make mistakes, only their spoiled riders.
	4. Learn to live below the poverty line.
	5. Invest in industrial-strength handcream.
	6. Go on the pill before major three-day events.
	7. Never wear a naff T-shirt with the legend 'Eventers do it 3 days running'.

in reflected glory. You will probably drive the gin palace lorry, wear the crested anoraks, and be very much 'part of the team'. Unfortunately, any mishaps can reflect on you also. You will always be loyal to your horses, and outwardly so to your rider. But should they make a cock-up on 'your' horse, you give them the silent treatment for a couple of days.

There is very little 'upstairs, downstairs' nonsense between riders and grooms, so your social life can also take a dramatic upturn.

'Beyond the Fringe' (Cambridge Footlights)

Blacksmith Having a well-shod horse is absolutely essential, so any rider must have a good rapport with the blacksmith. Obviously much farrier work is on non-competition horses, but smiths nevertheless deserve credit for any star performers in their care. One three-day event even gives a prize for the best-shod horse.

Vets If you have ambitions of becoming a vet and set your sights higher than budgies and guinea pigs, you could always specialise in horses. You are one of the most important people behind the competitive scene and it is a very 'hands on' (or often 'hands up') job. Of all people in the eventing world, you can actually make real money, enjoy the sport, and feel part of any success. The big disadvantage here is you need to be incredibly brainy. They say that it's made more difficult to qualify as a vet than as a doctor because animals can't tell you what's wrong with them.

First aid Although a doctor is always in attendance at an event, you can also participate by being one of the First Aid team. You may only be asked to cover one or two competitions a year, but it makes a change from bandage and kiss-of-life sessions every Wednesday night in the WI Hall. What's even better is that eventers do tend to fall off, so you might get some action.

Unless a rider is unconscious, however, the sight of a moonlighting dinner lady and her spotty sixteen-year-old assistant, running to their aid in weekend uniforms, is not reassuring. They would rather wait until the doctor arrives. Don't worry about this – it's a nice day out.

'The sight of a moonlighting dinner lady and her spotty assistant.'

Press If you can string a couple of words together (though it's not essential), you might like to try your hand at equestrian journalism. Horsey sports only tend to get onto the feature pages of national papers when one of the well-known participants has been caught in a compromising position – it makes good gossip ('upmarket', etc . . .), and a staff reporter will cover these stories. The 'quality' papers do give quite good coverage of eventing and the more upmarket tabloids might dedicate a couple of inches to a big competition. Even in the specialist press there is a fairly closed shop, but it's not impossible to break in.

Your best bet, to sample the undoubted delights of the press tent at a major competition, is to get yourself accredited to a local paper as a 'special' correspondent.

Oddly, the majority of equestrian writers have never ridden, but they probably know more about the sport than any of the riders. If you're going as a cub reporter, you will have to do a bit of homework. Get yourself introduced to one of the seasoned hacks and get chatting in the bar (free drinks). DON'T do this just before they are due to 'phone their copy in. It will take time for the riders to know who you are, and your exclusive interview may have to wait. Don't however, be intimidated by the stars. They like and need publicity and most of them are used to giving interviews.

The press are very well looked after at major trials. A team of PR girls keeps a scoreboard up to date, there is a closed-circuit TV, a comprehensive press pack, office facilities, and for a newcomer, lots of knowledgeable gossip and pontificating.

If you don't fancy writing, you could try your hand at photography. Your best way in there is to go to all the smaller events round the country and start snapping away. It's more difficult than it looks, but once you have cracked it, you can do quite well selling the prints to competitors.

'Senior competitors get a bit blasé.'

You will actually do better business at the most novice or junior competitions, as senior competitors get a bit blasé about photos.

Television The most closed shop to enter is becoming a TV pundit. Only the very top events are televised, and unless you are one of the brightest stars (cf how to become one), you will not be invited to impart your expert knowledge to the Nation. There is an outside chance of becoming the voice after the jazzed-up Mozart if you have served a long apprenticeship as a public address commentator. If you make it this far, there are several things you need to know:

Unlike a live audience at a horse trial, who will have some knowledge or interest in the sport, a *Grandstand* viewer at home has just been watching football and is waiting for the snooker. A problem that faces the producer is that all the scary jumps look quite easy on the box, so some excitement needs to be generated. Your style of delivery must also change completely. At a 'live' event, your audience can't see what is going on, so you are there to inform them, 'Number 25 is clear at the log'. A TV viewer can see this perfectly well, so you must 'comment' not 'state'.

The electronic set-up can also be quite intimidating. In front of you will be several monitor screens, with the centre one 'on air'. The producer may cut at any time, but your words should continue to flow. At the same time, the producer may be giving instructions over your headphones, and you have to resist answering him back. It's a bit like the trick of rubbing your tummy and patting your head at the same time.

The other possible job is to be the outdoor interviewer. Again, you will be wired for sound, but you must remember that your interviewee will either be on an emotional high or low. Incidentally, you don't get very well paid for any of this.

Sponsor Both riders and competitions need sponsors. Perhaps this is how you would like to get involved.

The most basic kind of sponsorship is being an indulgent parent and paying for your unemployable child's fun. As previous chapters have explained, this will be expensive. Once your darling has broken through into senior competition she may insist you change your name

to give her horses a more commercial prefix. Instead of
'Lucy Bratt on Mr Bratt's Lost Cause', she would prefer to
hear 'Lucy Bratt on Hampshire Crazy Investment Europe's
Lost Cause'. This will create the bogus impression that a
real company has sponsored her. Go along with this folly,
because it might help secure a genuine sponsor one day.

If you are not a parent of an aspiring eventer, but a
hitherto-successful and well-balanced businessman with
no connection with horses, what should possess you to
shell out good money for horse trials?

The usual answer is that you would like your product, or
company, to be associated with an 'upmarket . . .'

At the lowest level, all you would need to do is bung a few
quid to the organiser of your most local novice one-day
event in return for having one of the obstacles named after
your firm (Start-Rite Starter, etc). With perhaps two
hundred horses jumping it in a day, the commentator is
bound to give it a few mentions even if no one is listening.
You might get a decent lunch and a day out for your
troubles.

The next step, costing about one hundred times as
much, is to underwrite a complete competition. (Cf The
Henry Root Wet Fish Ltd Horse Trials.) Be warned,
however, that there is no such thing as a 'general public' at
ordinary events – your target must be the competitors and
helpers. If you think that the horse trials world is ready for
'wet fish', you might get a return on your investment, but it
will be impossible to quantify.

If, after a couple of years, you decide that you enjoy
hob-nobbing, and your 'wet fish' business has expanded
beyond your wildest dreams, it may be time to sponsor a
whole series of events which culminate in your showpiece
championship.

There is no more expensive way of becoming involved in
the sport than this. You need a very good reason. Perhaps

you are a rampant social climber – why not? If so, however, you may be disappointed, because you will by no means be the first – there are many more anoraks than tweeds these days.

On the other hand, you may originally have come into the sport by supporting an offspring, and instead of trying to get someone else to take over your financial burden, decide to increase their chances of recognition by becoming one of the game's principal benefactors. This has been tried before, and doesn't work.

Thirdly, and more sensibly, is the large corporate view. The money will be a drop in the ocean to a multinational but, being a businessman, you view the exercise in purely commercial terms. Your sales of four-wheel drive vehicles may not noticeably increase, but your championship horse trial, in a stately park, will provide a marvellous backdrop to entertain clients.

In the comfort of a large private marquee your guests can arrive for an elaborate buffet lunch and a constantly-open free bar. Top competitors are encouraged when possible to put in an appearance, and your clients never need leave the hospitality tent. In fact, many of them would be ill-advised to, since male guests tend to turn up in light suits and the ladies in crimplene cocktail frocks and peep-toed sling-back shoes.

The other approach is sponsoring an individual rider. This again can start in a modest way, but has its risks. The top performers who are likely to get your company mentioned on TV will require a king's ransom, but you may receive a glowing CV (see *passim*) from a local hopeful who 'just wants some help with the bills'. You know nothing about horse trials, but from the letter it looks as if the applicant has already booked her ticket to the next Olympics. This is light years away from the truth. In return for your modest generosity, however, she will be prepared

'She will be prepared to paint your name on her lorry.'

to paint your name on her lorry and also prefix her horses'
names with yours. The whole exercise can be quite fun,
because even minor successes can be celebrated. Don't
spoil it all by being too ambitious – your rider is unlikely to
make the grade.

Less of a risk, but at greater expense, is to support one of
the 'nearly' names. They will already have achieved a
certain amount and will be quite well known on the circuit.
You could achieve the same kudos as Lord Hesketh did in
launching James Hunt. It could almost cost you as much
money in the long run, too. Usually you won't have to buy
any horses, which is a relief, but enter into some sort of
leasing agreement. Riders like to retain overall ownership,
because their horses are usually their only tangible, and
sometimes considerable, asset. By leasing the animals, you

are also being patriotic. Up and coming nags with potential are often worth more than old ones who have won everything, but which have a lot of miles on the clock. A young rider with no job prospects, who is literally sitting on a fortune, will be tempted to sell it to a rich foreigner. You can't blame them.

Your outlay will almost match that of the senior competitors' deals. But your rider is now in the big time and less likely to win. Remember that the best you can hope for is a safe but spectacular fall on prime TV. This will be shown again in slow motion, and on the round up.

Your other investments will include the six-figure lorry, the 'team' padded anoraks, horse rugs bearing your logo, perhaps your own hospitality tent at competitions, and if your rider is really top-notch, you might also be expected to throw in a car plus phone for good measure. Since eventing is amateur (??!!) you will not pay a retainer to your jockey – but do expect substantial 'expenses' claims.

One of the cheekiest ways of latching onto the sport at the highest level, for the most publicity and least outlay, is to become the official sponsor of your product to the British Team. No risk here at all.

Sponsors	1. Throw your weight about, you are paying.
	2. Don't turn up in your Rolls-Royce, it will get bogged down.
	3. Your 'team' lorry must be bigger than everyone else's.
	4. Never give the slightest hint when you are about to withdraw your support.
	5. Try and persuade your corporate guests to dress half-appropriately.
	6. Enjoy the sycophancy from the tweedy brigade.

The team comes to a photo-call and puts on *your* boots, or breeches, hats, or jackets. The horses get togged up in saddles, bridles and rugs, with bags of branded feed in the foreground. Hey presto, and there's your advertising campaign for the year. That the riders will in fact use their favourite tried and tested kit, and their horses will continue with their usual diet, doesn't matter. For this scam, you may have to donate a few bob to central funds. It's cheap at the price.

The ruling body is always adamant that any sponsorship shouldn't alter the 'character' of the sport – don't you believe it.

10. 'Entertaining Mr Sloane' (Joe Orton)

If you have no desire to either ride in, or help at, horse trials, eventing could still become your sport. You could be a spectator. Don't underestimate your importance.

As you will have noticed, thousands of pounds are invested in the game. The protagonists want an audience. What they don't realise is that their sport will never have an instant appeal to the layman. This is for several reasons:

If, for example, you are the ultimate armchair sportsman, where considerable knowledge of several sports has been accumulated by watching *Grandstand*, horse trials would come low on your list of star attractions. Every other televised sport, from darts to athletics, football to snooker, keeps the audience's attention, because any move is instantly identifiable as a winning stroke or a cock-up. Even with other horse sports, the winner or losers can be identified by each action.

With the protracted nature of eventing, this isn't the case. In racing, the first past the post wins; in show jumping, the pole that comes down counts instantly; in polo, a winning goal is obvious.

With eventing, you have to wait to the end of the day to see where each competitor is standing. This of course dulls its television appeal, and is consequently seldom seen on the box.

Don't be put off by this. You can either don your bobble hat and scarf, support your local football team and get mugged on the way home, or spend your weekends following a sport which is 'upmarket . . .' on location.

The majority of twice-a-year enthusiasts only turn up at Burghley in the Autumn and Badminton in the Spring – a survivor's guide to these occasions will follow – but if you want to become an expert spectator, you will have to put in the odd day at your local run-of-the-mill events.

Here, at least, there will be no crowd problems, because there will be no crowd. On the other hand, you will be able to see all the top riders and horses competing in their warm-up events. Remember that horse trials is one of the few sports where we still do consistently well, so you could watch more than a dozen Olympic medallists and various World or European Champions performing.

A standard one-day event is a pleasant place to spend a Saturday or Sunday, and could easily provide you with the equivalent of seeing last year's Wimbledon champion playing on your local municipal courts. But don't expect any 'atmosphere'.

For this, you have to go to the two 'big ones'. Both are easy to get to: Burghley (September) is just off the A1, and Badminton (May) is off Junction 18 of the M4.

If you are going to indulge in a bi-annual interest in horse trials, there are several things you ought to know.

This is your guide to being a spectator:

If you are incredibly keen, you will want to spend the duration of the event on site. For this, you will either need to book into the public caravan area, or find a local pub to put you up. To book a room, you may well have to make arrangements a year in advance. Eventing isn't a 'popular' sport, but its two showcases have bigger crowds than most other sporting fixtures. Of course, a four-and-a-half mile course can accommodate this much more easily than an enclosed stadium.

If you have miraculously found a pub room, you check in on Wednesday morning. Otherwise, you tow your van into the 'grockle' park, get bogged down just by the entrance gate, and wait to be towed into position. You spend the next hour connecting the calor gas, discovering that your battery is flat for the electrics, and struggling with the awning where you will leave your muddy boots and assortment of dogs. At last you are organised, have attacked the bottle of sweet sherry and start thinking about making your way up to the house for the horse inspection. You then discover that one of your dogs is missing, and is consummating a relationship somewhere behind Row D22. Having eventually found Fifi, you zip her into the awning and march off towards the park, buying a programme on the way in.

You arrive to find that most people have got there before you, so you can't really see a thing. Flicking through the programme, you discover that a rider comes from just down the road from you and was in the same Pony Club as your daughter. This will be your 'one to follow'. Despite their name being in the programme, they haven't turned up, so you have to re-align your allegiances. You then find a horse with the same sire as your hunter. As it trots up in front of the panel, you say in a loud voice how much its head

resembles your old faithful. When it fails the initial test, you
ease away, saying in quiet tones that horses bred by 'Over
the Top' always 'move' like that, and 'it's unfair'. All that is
left is to marvel at the attire of the competitors as they lead
their horses up. Many of the girls actually wear skirts, and
become totally unrecognisable, and the men even wear
ties.

You go and pick up your dogs, come back to the park
and embark on your late-afternoon ramble round the
course. Several riders will be doing the same, so you can
glean bits of information to regale that night. When
someone in the next door caravan asks you what you think
about the water jump, you will confidently be able to reply
that the European Champion is going to take it 'on the left'
but that last year's winner 'fancies taking the short route' –
this will earn you considerable 'cred' points.

The next morning, you will go and watch the first day of
dressage. This will be very boring, but it has to be done. If
you really want to impress your caravan neighbours you
can even hire a set of headphones and hear an 'expert' talk
through each effort in technical detail. Your conversation
that evening can then include details, 'Yes, hers was a good
flowing test, but the impulsion in the counter-canter was
lacking and the horse was a bit over-bent in the half
passes.' That should do the trick.

If you are completely mad, you can repeat the
performance the next day, but you may well have become a
bore already. Go shopping instead. The trade stands at
major events are much more exciting than the competition.
You can buy almost anything from an expensive car, a
diamond tiara, all kinds of clothing, framed prints for the
loo, to practical jokes. An ever-popular item is the doggy
duvet, which of course is a nightmare to carry around for
the rest of the day.

Then comes Saturday. This is when the mega crowd

turns up. If you only have a passing interest in horse trials, this is the day for you.

Set your alarm early. Organise a proper picnic. Nothing too heavy: quiche, hard-boiled eggs, cold bangers and a decent supply of booze. Half an hour away from home, you will remember that you left the corkscrew behind. Three-quarters of an hour away, the children will start asking how much further it is to go. One hour from home, the dog will be sick over the picnic hamper.

At last you see signs to the event. Your journey has another hour to go. You are now doing five miles an hour, the children want to go to the loo, the car is over-heating, the dog is sick again, someone bashes your rear bumper and you get a warning from one of the stationed motorbike cops for abusive language.

At last you turn into the park and are directed to your parking spot by a maniac in a white coat.

First things first – find a loo. Rustic conveniences take on many forms. If you are so keen that you go to watch ordinary one-day events it is advisable to take nanny's advice and 'go' before you leave home.

If nature does, however, call during the day, there is an inescapable advantage of being a male of the species. Public loos at horsey do's have varying levels of sophistication:

1. The nearest bush.
2. A square, roofless screen of sackcloth, with ditch (for men) and a row of cut oildrums full of Elsan, furnished with seat for the girls. Make sure where the sun is, because you could easily find yourself performing a 'shadow' silhouette show.
3. A single zip-fronted mini tent with a chemical bucket. These have been known to blow down in the wind, leaving you embarrassingly exposed.

'A single zip-fronted mini tent.'

4. (What you find at major three-day events). Specially-
   erected wooden squares which can accommodate
   urinals and sit-downs. The urinals consist of a raised
   pig trough, tilted towards a deep ditch below the
   sit-downs. The sit-downs are like mediaeval
   commodes, a wooden box with a hole. Down below is
   the ditch. If you lose your signet ring down there, *leave
   it.* You will also inevitably discover that the paper has
   run out. Whatever your luck, you will emerge smelling
   of creosote, which may well be a blessing.
5. Some kind of sophistication has been introduced:
   the portable flushing loo. These are by no means
   universal, and are usually blocked anyway.
6. Under no circumstances use the loo in your caravan.
   Go to a local pub, or anything, but a long weekend's

enjoyment will be surely ruined by returning home on a Sunday night and having to deal with the 'slopping out'.

Once you have sampled the loos at the big event, it's time for the picnic.

Scrape the dog sick off the hamper, unfold the tartan rug, tie the pooch to the bumper and pretend to enjoy yourself.

Now is the time to start showing your 'knowledge' by predicting who could go well. After lunch, you also want to go to the loo. You will meet the family at the scoreboard. This is the time to remember where you have parked your car. The experts tie a balloon to the aerial, but if everyone did this you would still be lost.

Eventually you find your family again, and you are all keen to start walking round the course to see some action. Your wife in the meantime will have spotted something on a trade stand which she wants you to buy, and the children are starting to grizzle. A row then ensues, but eventually you get your way and a five-mile walk is in order.

If you have any mini-children, you can dump them off at a crèche, since under no circumstances do you want to push a baby buggy over grass and mud for the next two hours. Look in your programme to see where the course starts. It is Phase D you are after – don't religiously start walking round the ten miles of roads and tracks (see *passim*), you will miss everything. The general flow starts at fence one, sees a horse over it and moves on round the course. If you are an individualist, however, you go in reverse.

Only if you walk the course on the earlier days can you really show your 'knowledge', by pacing out the jumps and remarking in a loud voice that there are three strides between elements one and two, and that you would take it at a forty-five degree angle. This will sound impressive to anyone within earshot, unless they happen to be a competitor, who will know you are talking complete nonsense.

On the Saturday, you won't get within fifty yards of the jump, and the most you are likely to see is the rider's helmet bobbing up as it goes over the fence. If you then fail to see it on the landing side and hear an 'oooh' from the crowd, you can safely assume 'yer man' has fallen off. You can keep up your cred, however, by dropping remarks about how your hunter jumped a similar obstacle last season. You can also win points by referring to top riders by their Christian names, as if they were your closest friends.

You might find it odd that a sport which has almost no public appeal at its everyday level pulls in massive crowds at the two British showpieces. This is peculiar to Britain. Even at World and Olympic championships abroad, very few people bother to turn out to watch. The big crowds at Burghley and Badminton have nothing whatever to do with the popularity of 'eventing' (a point which you should remember if you are considering becoming a sponsor). They are both just a great family day out in the country. The opportunity to have the run of a stately park, the chance of 'Royalty spotting', and the best tented shopping area you are ever likely to find. Even if you leave the picnic at home by mistake there are so many eateries and places to get a drink that you can spend the whole week there without ever having to bother to see a horse.

There are stands selling toasted sandwiches, baked spuds, roast pork, popcorn and candy floss. You can go more upmarket in the sea food tent where crab, prawns, lobster and champagne awaits – at a price – or just go to one of the public bars to drink pints of beer out of plastic beakers. Unfortunately, most of the bars are staffed by dim female teenagers; equally slow, but more pleasant, older ladies with dyed black hair; or mincing provincial poofs. Never mind, you get your drink eventually.

You can wear pretty much what you like as a spectator, and if you feel incorrectly attired you will be able to buy the gear at the event to suit any image. Under no circumstances, however, wear riding clothes (which some people do!). You will look ridiculous, and walking all day in rubber riding boots will give you the blisters you deserve.

To avoid getting stuck in a jam on the way out it's sensible to leave before the last horse goes. You can always catch up by watching the TV on Sunday.

If you become a complete eventing groupie, you could even spend your hard-earned holidays by going on trips to support the team at International Championships. You will really have arrived as a spectator, and by now the top riders probably even know you. You will be expected to help the team at the trials by reporting back to base how various fences are being negotiated, and may even get in on some of the parties. You can consider yourself an integral part of the Nation's international success, without ever having to have sat on a horse. You can even pay a fee and become an official supporter and wear an enamel Union Jack badge. Wow!

Spectator	1. Remember the corkscrew.
	2. Remember where you have left the car.
	3. Do not drop your keys while going round the course.
	4. Leave the dogs at home.
	5. Leave the children at home.
	6. Leave your credit card at home.
	7. Watch it all on closed-circuit TV in a tent.
	8. Watch it on your own TV at home.

So – now armed with all this knowledge, you can become involved with horse trials in whichever role takes your fancy.

It may cost you a fortune, it may cost you nothing, or it could even provide you with a modest income. But above all, you will be part of a sport whose 'upmarket country image' can do wonders for your social standing. You can't lose.